Golf Swing
BASICS

Golf Swing
BASICS

· · · · · · · · · · ·

Oliver Heuler

Sterling Publishing Co., Inc.   New York

Translated by Elisabeth Reinersmann

Library of Congress Cataloging-in-Publication Data
Heuler, Oliver.
    [Schwung. English]
    Golf swing basics / by Oliver Heuler ; [translated by Elisabeth
Reinersmann].
        p.   cm.
    Includes index.
    ISBN 0-8069-3878-1
    1. Swing (Golf).   2. Golf.   I. Title.
GV979.S9H47813   1996
796.352'3—dc20   95-49272
                                                            CIP

10 9 8 7 6 5 4 3 2 1

Published 1996 by Sterling Publishing Company, Inc.
387 Park Avenue South, New York, N.Y. 10016
Originally published by Falken-Verlag GmbH
under the title *Der Schwung*
© 1994 by Falken-Verlag GmbH, 65527 Niedernhausen/Ts.
English translation © 1996 Sterling Publishing Co., Inc.
Distributed in Canada by Sterling Publishing
% Canadian Manda Group, One Atlantic Avenue, Suite 105
Toronto, Ontario, Canada M6K 3E7
Distributed in Great Britain and Europe by Cassell PLC
Wellington House, l25 Strand, London WC2R 0BB, England
Distributed in Australia by Capricorn Link (Australia) Pty Ltd.
P.O. Box 6651, Baulkham Hills, Business Centre, NSW 2153, Australia
Printed and bound in Hong Kong
All rights reserved

Sterling ISBN 0-8069-3878-1

FOREWORD

In recent years, golf instruction has become increasingly complicated. The purpose of the golf swing, however, remains the same: to swing the clubhead accurately, time after time, through the ball. Therefore, the flight of the ball should always be the first consideration in improving a golf swing. From this it is possible to conclude what the club is doing at impact, and what the golfer is doing to affect the flight of the ball.

In the last decade, the video camera has become a valuable tool in golf instruction. Oliver Heuler has made good use of this technology in teaching, but it should never be forgotten that the aim is not to make perfect-looking swings, but to create the proper impact of club on ball. My aim has always been to correct the flight of the ball by improving and simplifying the golf swing. In achieving that, the plane on which the clubshaft travels plays the most important role in my teaching.

This book provides a detailed description of the swing plane, which will certainly help you in your game. High-quality drawings and photographs of the proper swing will help you to understand what is really important in golf. In the past, Oliver has travelled and discussed golf with all the great instructors, including John Jacobsa, Denis Pugh, and Michael Hebron. Along with his own experiences, these talks moulded his teaching philosophy, which is very similar to my own.

I wish Oliver and his most promising student, Marc Amort—both former students—good luck in their golf careers. Finally, I hope that this book will lead to a better understanding of the golf swing and will improve your game.

Dallas, July 1994

Hank Haney
Owner and Director of Golf at Hank Haney Golf Ranch, McKinney, Texas, and Hank Haney Cityplace Golf Center, Dallas. Teacher of over 100 touring professionals including Tommy Armour III, Mark O'Meara, Chip Beck, and Bruce Crampton.

CONTENTS

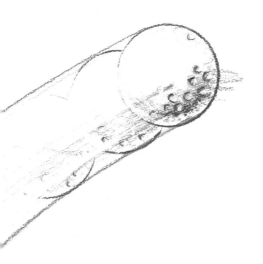

CONTENTS

The aim of the swing is to consistently hit a golf ball at high speed with the sweet spot and with the clubface pointing towards the target.

INTRODUCTION

When I ask golfers, even experienced ones, to tell me about the problems they're having, most of them say, "I hit the ball too fast and with too much power," or "I always start the downswing with my shoulders instead of turning my hips." These answers are a sure indication that many players have no clear understanding about what is really important in golf. When I then ask what allows a ball to travel straight through the air over a long distance, they reply, "The left arm must be straight, and the head must stay down."

However, I can state what is really important in one sentence, and in such a way that everyone understands: *The clubface, pointing towards the target, must hit the ball with high speed on the sweet spot.*

Generally speaking, how a golfer is able to achieve this is irrelevant, as long as the golfer can repeat the swing over and over again. Obviously, we cannot ignore certain specific techniques and basic rules, but we should discuss them only after we consider those factors that influence the ball at the moment of impact.

How do we find out what went wrong at the moment of impact? If no video camera is available (used with very low exposure time and single-frame stops), and if a player does not have access to a computerized image of the moment of impact, only the behavior of the ball provides the needed information about what kind of mistakes the golfer made.

The divot and whether or not the club rotated in the hands, and if so, how much, yield additional information. The ball only reacts to what happens in the last milliseconds before the clubhead makes contact with it. An advanced player needs to be able to interpret the flight of a ball correctly, because only when the player understands how the ball behaves can he know what the club did at the moment of impact. Only then can the player determine what was responsible for the mistakes before or during the swing.

A word to left-handed golfers: I prepared this book, including the photographs, from a right-hander's perspective. Lefties need to look at the mirror image of the photos; also, whenever there is a reference to a particular side, left-handed golfers should just visualize it in reverse.

9

Four factors, often a combination of several components, determine how and in what direction a ball will fly. A ball reacts to these factors, regardless of the combination in which they occur.

The most important factor is the **position of the clubface at the moment of impact**. For the ball to travel straight towards the target, the face of the club must point in the direction of the target. The

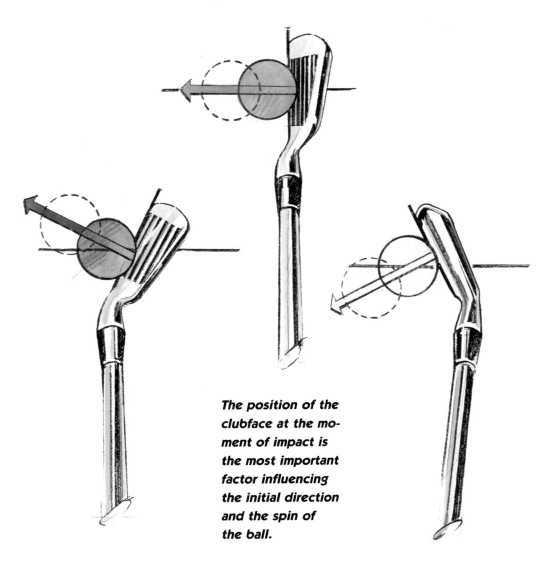

The position of the clubface at the moment of impact is the most important factor influencing the initial direction and the spin of the ball.

leading edge of the club points vertically to the target and is parallel to the ground.

This factor is primarily responsible for the initial direction and the rotation of the ball. For example, assuming that all other factors are correct, if the clubface is off by only 5 degrees (open) when it hits the ball, the ball will initially take off 4 degrees to the right and travel even farther to the right during the flight. With a long club, the ball will travel even farther to the right; with a shorter club, the turn to the right will be less because the point of impact is lower, and the club travels at a lower speed.

If the heel of the club is farther away from the ground than the tip, the vertical plane points to the right rather than in the direction of the target. If all other factors are correct, the ball will veer farther to the right initially and during its flight.

Furthermore, the face of the club must reach the ball at its loft. This means that the end of the grip (viewed from the front) must be above the face of the club at the moment of impact. In other words, the end of the grip should not be either in front or behind, because these positions increase or reduce the loft of the club, reducing or increasing the flight curve.

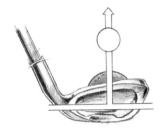

The lie of the golf club at the moment of impact influences the direction of the clubface (left).

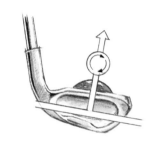

The dynamic loft (the loft at the moment of impact) influences how high the ball will go (below).

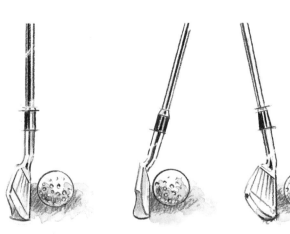

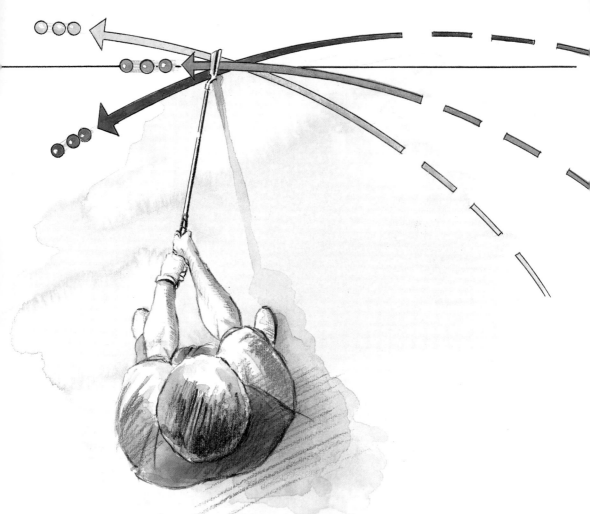

The second factor influencing the initial direction of a ball is the angle of approach of the clubhead. Since the player stands alongside and not above the ball, the club moves to the inside at the backswing (towards the player), moves (towards the ball) from the inside-out at the downswing, and to the inside (towards the player) at the follow-through. The club-face points towards the target at the moment of impact. If the club travels from the outside-in, "through" the ball, the ball will start out towards the left (if all other factors are correct) and then veer slightly to the right during the flight. This is the *horizontal angle of impact*, also called the "swinging plane of the club."

Since the ball is on the ground, the club moves up during the backswing, down during the downswing, and up again during and-after the follow-through.

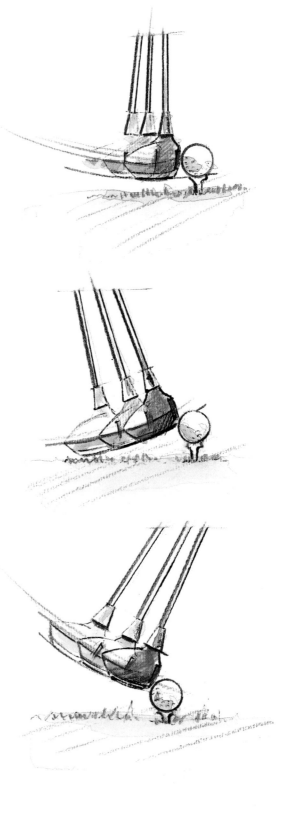

The vertical angle of impact influences the way a ball starts out and the height of the flight.

The result is the *vertical angle of impact*. Under ideal circumstances, this angle is relatively flat. When using an iron, the club hits the ball while still in the downward movement, and, when using a wood, the ball hits at the exact moment when the club is parallel to the ground. If the angle of impact is too steep at the moment of impact, the club is moving too far towards the ground, and the force of the hit doesn't move towards the target, causing low hits when teeing-off with a wood. If, on the other hand, the angle is too flat when hitting without a tee, particularly when the ball is in a bad position, the player will encounter a lot of problems, because the lowest point of the swing (from the player's perspective) is to the right of the ball.

13

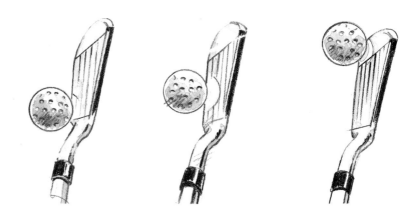

The third important factor is that the club must hit the ball with the sweet spot of the clubface. Just as is true on a tennis racket, one spot on the face of the golf club transfers the energy of movement most effectively to the ball. This is the sweet spot. If, for instance, the heel of the club hits the ball, the grip in the player's hands rotates counterclockwise, depriving the ball of some of its energy. If the club hits the ball above the sweet spot, the clubhead moves too close to the ground, and the ball travels a much shorter distance. Hitting the ball vertically with the sweet spot guarantees the size of the divot.

The speed of the clubhead is very important, but it is not the only determining factor. Any incorrect factor will shorten the distance a ball travels.

These four factors, influencing the way you hit the ball, are the keys to a successful golf game. If you want to improve your game, you must be able to figure out how your moment of impact differs from the ideal. In general, mistakes run in patterns, meaning that they are much alike. For instance, a player rarely alternates between pull/slice and push/hook hits.

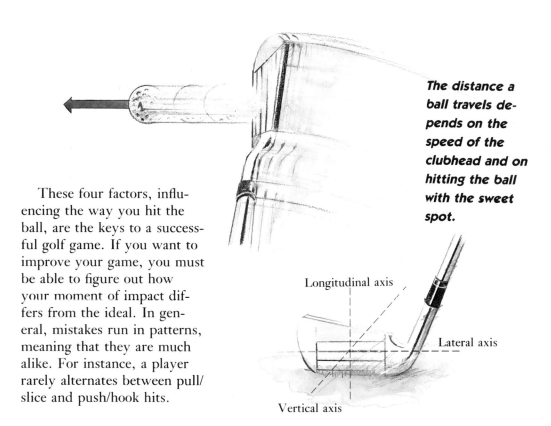

The distance a ball travels depends on the speed of the clubhead and on hitting the ball with the sweet spot.

Longitudinal axis

Lateral axis

Vertical axis

Factors Influencing the Moment of Impact

Factor		Description	Possibilities
Clubface	Vertical axis	Position of clubface	Clubface pointing: to the right, directly at, to the left of the target
	Longitudinal axis	Dynamic club lie	Heel of club pointing into the air, lower edge parallel to the ground, tip of club pointing into the air
	Lateral axis	Dynamic loft	Club loft at the moment of impact (according to the position of the club): stronger, weaker
Angle of attack	Horizontal	Swinging plane	Swinging plane: outside-in, inside-in, inside-out
	Vertical	Angle of impact	Angle of impact: from below up, from above down
Point of impact	Horizontal	Sweet spot	Hit with: heel of club, sweet spot, top of club
	Vertical	Proper divot size	Size of divot: too thin, proper size, too fat
Speed	Relative to the angle of attack	Speed of the clubhead	Clubhead: too slow, right speed, too fast

Geometry of the Swing

In this chapter I want to introduce you to the basic elements of geometry that influence a good swing. Successful golfers never violate geometry. Since it is impossi-

Therefore, if the club swings in a circular fashion on an angle around your body, it will move away from the target line and towards the inside, in the direction of the

Since the ball is to one side, the club moves through the ball from the inside-in . . .

ble to stand directly over the ball when swinging a golf club, you have to stand to the right or to the left of it, depending on whether you are right-handed or left-handed.

player. During the backswing it will travel from the inside closer to the target, and, after the impact, it will again swing inside. Several problems arise if the club moves through the ball from the inside-out or from the outside-in. This is why I recommend that you not try to hold the club over the target line as long as possible. Only at the time of impact does the clubhead point for a brief moment directly towards the target.

A correct swing is one that moves the clubhead through the ball from the inside-in. When using a wood, the curve of the swing will be greater than when using an iron. This is because the shaft is longer, increasing the distance between the player and the ball.

Since the ball is on the ground, the club moves up at the backswing, down during the downswing, and up again during the follow-through. At the moment of impact, the clubhead should be at the vertex of the swing. When using an iron, the vertex might be slightly to the left of the ball (from the player's point of view). Try not to swing upwards through the ball to lift the ball in the air. This lift happens automatically because of the loft of the club (due to the position of the clubface).

. . . and during the course of the swing upwards, it moves down and up again.

17

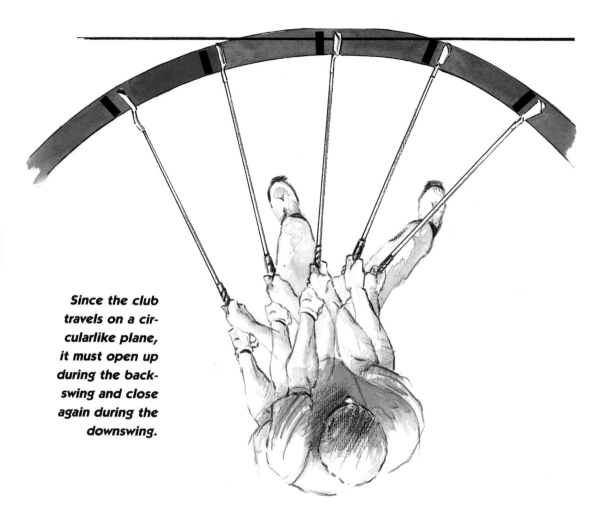

Since the club travels on a circularlike plane, it must open up during the backswing and close again during the downswing.

Because it isn't possible for the clubhead to travel on a straight plane, it is also impossible for the clubface to remain vertical to the target line during the whole course of the swing. With an inside-in swing, the clubface will automatically open during the backswing and close again during the downswing. In other words, the club will only be vertical to the target at the start of the swing.

In order to hit straight, many players try to keep the club straight as long as possible. But this is a contradiction because a clubface that is travelling in a circularlike arc on an angle cannot approach the ball straight on with high speed.

Consistency of a Swing

Previously I stated that it does not matter how the golf club approaches a ball, as long as the result is consistent rather than one satisfying swing here and there. The goal should be to hit the golf ball successfully and consistently.

The basic rule for a successful swing is an uncomplicated movement that you can repeat at any time. Over the long haul, complicated and unnecessary movements are difficult to repeat.

The goal is to take into account all the factors that influence the behavior of the ball at the moment of impact and to do so as simply and as effectively as possible. The most decisive elements here are the plane in which the clubhead moves and the movements of the player's body. In order to eliminate unnecessary, compensating movements during the swing, the plane that the shaft assumes at the address position must be the same throughout the swing. The easiest way to assure this is to keep the spine in the same position throughout the swing.

In order to comprehend the following discussion about techniques, you must fully understand the basics we discussed in this chapter.

During the course of the swing, the plane of the club and the position of the player's spine should never change.

INTRODUCTION

THE GRIP

The golfer must have a proper grip for the club-face to be straight at the moment of impact and for the proper flexing of the wrists. These, in turn, influence the direction and the distance the ball will travel.

When you grip a golf club, remember that the grip is a deciding factor in the orientation of the face of the club at the moment of impact. In fact, it is the most important factor at the moment of impact. If a golfer rotates his hands, the clubface will be off center when it reaches the ball and won't travel in the intended direction. In addition, gripping the club improperly also leads to an improper flexing of the wrists, and this is the most important factor in moving the clubhead at high speed.

In spite of the fact that a proper grip determines the direction and length of a hit, most players, at every level of golf competition, neglect this most basic factor.

Many golfers think the grip is boring and unimportant. They blame their mistakes on the way they swing the club.

However, an improper grip never leads to a correct swing because, in order to hit the ball straight on, a player has to perform all kinds of compensating, complicated movements during the swing. For example, the technique Chip Beck uses won't do much good if a player does not grip the club exactly the same way he does.

Let me begin by describing the basic concept involved for achieving a correct grip. Then I'll explain two details that you can use to make individual adjustments, because there is no such thing as a universally applicable grip.

Basic Technique

Place the club diagonally across the inside of the left hand.

The technique for gripping the handle of a club discussed in the following pages has been proven to work. It is the best guarantee that the clubface will consistently hit the ball correctly.

Left Hand
Hold the club in your left hand so that the grip crosses

the first segment of your index finger and the base rests against the ball of your hand. To do this properly, let your arm hang down relaxed alongside your body, curl your fingers, and let the club "fall" into them.

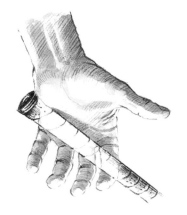

The fingers hold the club from below, while the ball of the hand holds it from above.

Hold the club with the left hand alongside the left side of the body.

The balls of the hand and thumb and the thumb itself will then automatically be on top of the handle. Hold the club between the balls of the hand, the ball of the thumb, and the thumb from above and with the fingers from below, so that the end of the

thumb position assures you that the club will not swing back too far, because the "shorter" the position of the thumb on the handle, the shorter the backswing. The "longer" the position of the thumb, the more restricted the movements of the wrist

handle is visible. (Some handles have a ring near the end.)

Place the left thumb slightly right of center on top of the handle. To find the proper place for the thumb, stretch the thumb down the handle as far as possible and remember that spot. Pull the thumb back as far as you can and remember that spot also. The correct position for the thumb is exactly halfway between these two spots. This

will be. If hooking is a problem for you, a grip adjustment to the latter position may be very helpful.

When you place the club exactly in the middle and in front of the body (the lower front edge of the clubhead pointing upwards), and you don't rotate the clubhead, the knuckles of the index and middle fingers are visible in the neutral grip. The V created by the thumb and the upper edge of the hand (the extension of the index finger) points to the middle of the right collarbone in the neutral grip. If there are more knuckles or fewer knuckles visible, you have rotated your hand too far to the right or to the left, respectively. From this perspective, along the whole

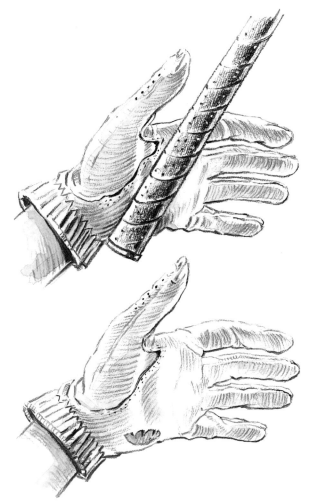

length of the hand, the end of the handle should not be visible. If it is, you have rotated your hand too far to the left or the ball of your little finger is to the left of the handle instead of on top. In the latter case, the grip is between the ball of the little finger and the ball of the thumb instead of underneath and below both. Flexing the wrist is extremely difficult, and you usually rotate your hand too far to the left, causing the ball to slice.

A sure sign that this is a problem is that your glove always wears out at the ball of the hand.

A good cure is to make sure that you always grip the handle in your left hand with your arm extended alongside your body.

If you hold the club handle at too much of an angle, your glove will usually wear out in the area of the ball of your hand.

THE GRIP

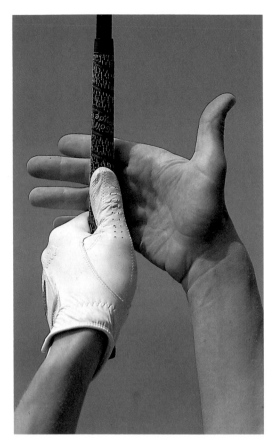 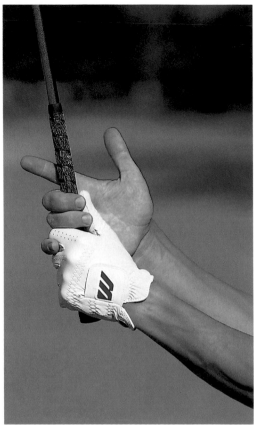

Place the middle and ring fingers of your right hand against the grip from underneath (above left), closing them against the thumb (right).

Right Hand

When you place your right hand on your left hand, hold the club directly in front of your body. Place your middle and ring fingers at the spots on the handle that are exactly opposite your left thumb.

As you close the fingers around the handle, their tips should touch the left thumb at its left side. To create an overlapping grip, place the right little finger in the space between the index and middle fingers of the left hand. Place the inside of the right hand on top of the left thumb so that the ball of the right thumb rests on top of the left thumb. The ball of the little finger of the right hand rests on the right side of the left thumb. The left thumb rests in the hollow space between the ball of the right hand and thumb, totally covered by the right hand. The left thumb

comes to rest at the left side of the handle. Place the right index finger, slightly splayed out, on the right side of the handle. (Slightly splayed out means that the right index finger and the right middle finger do not touch each other, creating a small space between them.) The thumb and index finger are touching each other at the joint of the thumb. At the left side of the grip, the right index finger and the thumb, depending on the length of your finger, will touch each other almost or just slightly. In this position, the right thumb cannot exert any negative influence. Many golfers, however, find that their thumbs slide to the top of the handle and then do exert pressure on the club. In addition, the whole hand rotates too far to the right.

The complete grip: the drawing (left) is from the player's perspective (two knuckles of the right hand are visible). The photo (above) shows the position viewed from the front.

THE GRIP

Position the backs of both hands at a 30-degree angle to each other. Holding the handle so that your hands are parallel to each other (as when you clap your hands) is wrong from a physiological point of view and interferes with the flexibility of your wrists. If you bend your upper body slightly forward and let your arms hang down without any tension, you will notice that if you place the upper edges of your hands next to each other, the backs of your hands almost form a right angle. That is why the hands gripping the handle rotate slightly against each other.

Counting the number of knuckles that are visible only makes sense from this perspective and only when the head is absolutely still.

When you let your arms hang down without any tension, the back of your hands form a right angle.

You can test your right hand, as you just did with your left hand. Hold the club in front of your body. You should be able to see the knuckles of your index and middle fingers without moving your head, assuming you are using the neutral grip. From this perspective, the middle joint of your right index finger and the tip of your right thumb are parallel to each other. Your thumb and index finger create a V, which points to the right collarbone (again, assuming you are using a neutral grip).

Both hands must form a single unit because they have to participate in the swing in equal measure. Using this grip, you should easily be able to lift the club off the ground by simply flexing your wrists (radial flexion). With the club in an elevated position, the angle between your lower arm and the club shaft should be about 90 degrees.

When holding the club correctly, you can easily lift the club off the ground just by flexing your wrists.

The further to the left or right you place your hands on the handle of the club, the more likely it is that the ball will veer to the opposite side.

Since the grip is the deciding factor for the position of the clubface at the moment of impact, you have to adjust the rotation of the hands on the handle according to the flight path the ball is to assume. For example, a beginner, whose clubface does not close enough, cannot grip the handle the same way a tour professional, who is trying to keep his ball from hooking, can. However, individual adjustments must stay within certain limits because adjusting the grip won't correct every incorrect flight pattern. Start with the neutral grip: the grip in which the Vs of both hands point approximately towards the middle of the collarbone. If the flight pattern of the ball indicates that the grip is not closing the clubface enough (in other words, that the ball almost always veers to the right), rotate both hands to the right until the Vs point to the right shoulder. If in a neutral grip the ball veers to the left, rotate your hands until the Vs point to your chin.

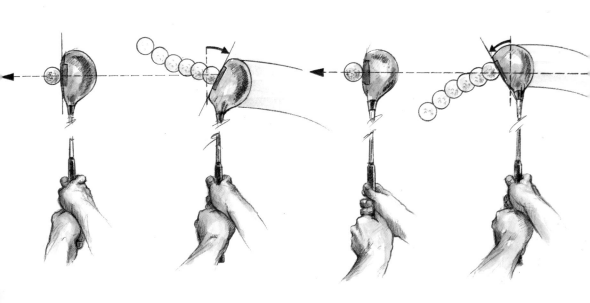

The second adjustment involves the little finger of the right hand. Golfers with small hands often have a problem with the overlapping grip (the right little finger rests in the space between the index and middle finger) because the finger seems to constantly slip out of position. If this is the case, the player may consider using the interlocking grip (used by Jack Nicklaus and Tom Kite), in which the fingers of both hands interlock. If you have small hands, this grip guarantees that your hands will stay together. However, because the little finger of your right hand hooks around the index finger of your left hand, you need to make sure that your right hand does not slide too far to the right.

For children and players with extremely small hands, this alternative grip might still not work. If this is the case, consider the ten-finger grip. (We also call this the baseball grip, even if the term is not quite correct because you hold a baseball bat in the palm of the hands while you hold a golf club inside the fingers.) All the fingers touch the handle, and the right little finger and the left index finger touch each other.

To use the overlapping grip, place the little finger in the space where the index finger and the middle finger of the left hand touch each other.

With the interlocking grip, the fingers of both hands hook into each other.

With the ten-finger grip, also known as the baseball grip, every finger touches the handle of the club.

THE GRIP

Grip Tension

No matter if you are a beginner, just learning how to hold a club, or if you are an experienced player, changing over to the techniques just discussed, a new grip feels awkward and even uncomfortable. Despite the fact that your new grip is correct, it feels worse. However, with patience and consistency, you will become used to the new grip, usually sooner rather than later.

Your hands may cramp from the new position. We don't want this to happen when you are holding a golf club because hand cramps may prevent your wrists from moving freely when you swing a club.

The optimum tension is the one that holds the club only tightly enough so that it doesn't slide out of your hands. The tension increases during the swing, so the danger of not gripping tightly enough is very small (for the exception, see page 34, "Grip During the Swing"). Gripping the club too tightly, even with a correct grip, may lead to slicing the ball, because the club might stay too far behind the hands during the downswing. (Hesitating while opening the angle between the left arm and the

The optimal pressure is the one that prevents the club from sliding out of your hands.

shaft does not allow the clubhead to catch up with the hands soon enough.)

The reason the clubface rotates at the moment of impact is not because of a loose grip, but because you didn't hit the ball with the sweet spot. Such a hit produces enough force that even a club held tightly won't prevent the clubface from rotating.

If the clubface rotates to the left during the swing, the heel of the clubhead hits the ball; if the clubface rotates to the right, the tip hits the ball.

Left Hand
Contrary to popular opinion, the left hand does not exert pressure with the last three

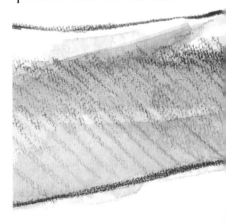

fingers (middle to little finger). Mainly it exerts pressure with the index finger and the ball of the little finger. Since you hold the club handle diagonally in the palm of your hand, you hold it in place with both. Pressure will increase automatically when the pulling force increases, since you hold the club in a "self-restricted position." The left thumb, which receives the most pressure at the highest point of the backswing, prevents the club from swinging too far back.

Right Hand

The middle and ring finger of the right hand exert the greatest pressure on the handle. The thumb and index fingers press against each other only slightly at the joint of the thumb. Even though you have the greatest amount of feeling in these two fingers, you should never exert force consciously. The little finger, too, should rest passively on the left hand.

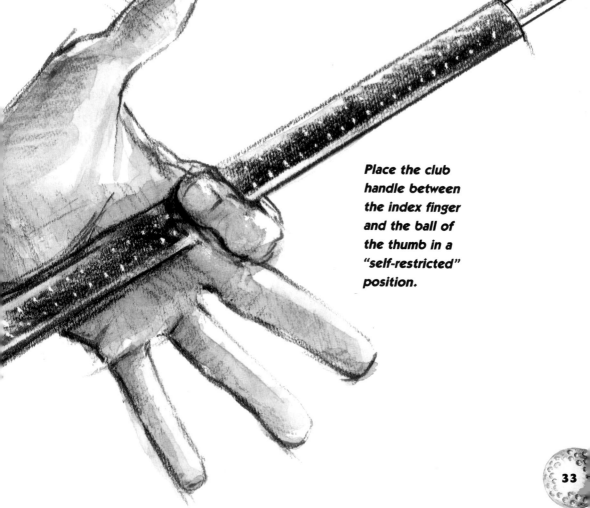

Place the club handle between the index finger and the ball of the thumb in a "self-restricted" position.

33

Grip During the Swing

The grip should never change during the swing. However, the danger of loosening occurs primarily in three different places, most often at the highest point of the backswing:

▶ At the point where the ball of the little finger of the left hand touches the club handle
▶ Where the ball of the right thumb and left thumb make contact
▶ At the point where right thumb and index finger make contact

In theory, you do not have to change your grip after a successful hit. But when practising on the range, you should release your grip after each hit. I recommend this for two reasons:

▶ To avoid unnecessary cramping of your hand
▶ To constantly practise proper grip techniques

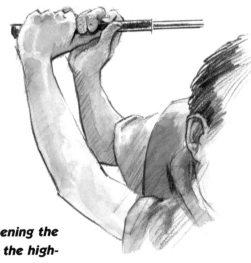

Loosening the grip at the highest point of the backswing lets the clubhead swing too far back.

In order to prepare for a good swing, you should practise grip techniques every day. You do not need to be on the golf course, you can easily practise your grip at home.

The Grip

....

▶ *The grip controls the direction of the clubface and makes the flexion of the wrists possible.*

▶ *The club handle rests in the left hand between the fingers on one side, and the thumb and ball of the thumb and the palm on the other side. Mainly, it is the fingers of the right hand that hold the handle.*

▶ *With a neutral grip, the Vs point to the right collarbone.*

▶ *The pressure exerted is not more than it would be for a handshake.*

....

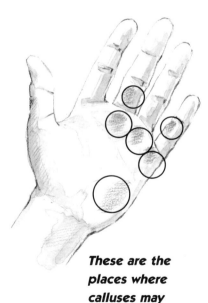

These are the places where calluses may appear, even with a correct grip.

Even after a player masters the perfect grip, he may have to deal with calluses on his left hand. Beginners and players who spend a lot of time practising are particularly prone to calluses. To protect themselves, most golfers wear a glove on the left hand. A glove for the right hand is not necessary because there is only limited contact between the fingers and the handle. The drawing on the left shows where calluses may develop with a correct grip.

POSTURE AND STANCE

A player must
have good pos-
ture and the cor-
rect stance in
order to move his
arms and club on
the proper plane.
These, in turn, lead
to the angle of
attack and the
ability to hit the
ball with the
sweet spot.

If you don't bend your upper body, the golf club will not reach the ground.

You have learned that the grip is responsible for the position of the clubface at the moment of impact. Your posture and stance determine the plane on which the club travels (the vertical and horizontal angle of attack, which are the factors that influence the initial flight path of the ball and the height the ball will reach).

Although many would reverse the order, I will discuss posture before talking about the stance. I believe the former to be much more important than the elements influencing the stance, not the least because players make most of their mistakes in posture.

Posture

When you first watched golfers playing, I am sure you must have wondered why they take on such a peculiar posture just before they get ready to hit the ball. The reason may not be immediately obvious, but after closer inspection, it becomes rather clear.

I invite you to try the following experiment: Hold a 6 iron in your hands (as discussed in the previous chapter) and stand absolutely straight. Let your arms hang down and you will notice that the club does not reach the ground.

In order to play with this club, you must try to make yourself shorter. A beginner instinctively bends his back until the club reaches the ground. This, of course, allows him to hit the ball, but he won't be able to remain in this position during the full backswing. For this reason, the beginner will abandon this posture during the backswing and straighten his back. During the downswing, he must again bend his back to the same degree, something that requires considerable skill and coordination and, over the long haul, is not really possible. Since the degree the upper body bends dictates the plane in which the shoulders move (and, by extension, also the plane of the arms and the club), we need to pay a lot of attention to this factor.

By bending both the knees and the hips, the player becomes shorter, producing a posture he can maintain during the swing and establishing the proper plane of the swing.

A beginner usually allows a club to reach the ground by bending his back.

POSTURE AND STANCE

 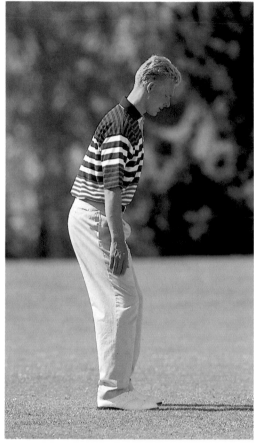

Angle of the Knees

The angle of the knees is the angle created by the thighs and lower legs. However, in golf it is not correct to "bend your knees" as that phrase is commonly understood. Actually, the golfer should "bend his thighs." He does this by bending his knees without pushing the knees forward to any appreciable degree. He lowers his buttocks until he forms a straight line between the head of his thigh bone (the head of the femur) and his heels. Both his knees are then directly over the balls of his feet, balancing the weight of his body on his heels. Properly bending his hips allows him to correct this poor posture.

In golf, you don't "bend your knees" (far left), *instead you "bend your thighs"* (middle) *without bringing your knees forward to any appreciable degree.*

The hip bones are above the heels, and the shoulders are above the knees and the balls of the feet.

Angle of the Hips

The angle of the hips is the angle created by bending the upper body and the thighs. In the position described above, the player is bending his upper body forward from the hips until (viewed from the side) the back portion of his shoulders is vertically in line with both knees. The player must make sure that he doesn't bend his back too far or that his back becomes hollow. He must be careful not to change the position of the lower part of his body. He bends his spine forward at a 30–35-degree angle. The upper body may bend less, so that the shoulders are above the knees and the balls of the feet, but the weight of the body must balance equally between the heels and the balls of the feet.

 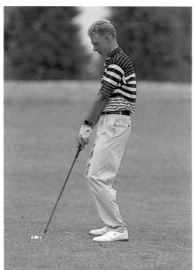

When the legs are too straight, the upper body must bend down too far (position too far from ball).

When the upper body is too straight, the knees must bend too far (position too close to ball).

Assume that the golfer will only use the posture we just discussed for learning, and that as soon as he masters it, he won't use it anymore. Since it is not all that easy for the untrained athlete to achieve the proper posture, we recommend that beginners stand alongside a mirror. Beginners believe at the outset that the recommended posture is unnatural. Another part of the reluctance to learn this posture is that players think they look silly if they assume the proper position. This experience is much like sitting on a chair: sitting with a straight back seems uncomfortable and unnatural. When we assume a comfortable position (sliding forward and bending the back), we have

really chosen a position that isn't good for our spine and is not very aesthetic. Compare the posture of a golfer with straight legs and a bent back to one who has assumed the proper posture, and you will have to admit that the latter gives a much more aesthetically pleasing picture.

This does not mean that the correct posture in golf is necessarily comfortable. In the beginning, most players feel tension in the upper part of the lumbar region. The tension is simply a sign that the particular musculature in this area is being used. In time, and with continued practice, the tension will disappear. With the proper posture, the muscle tension gives the player a feeling of being

"charged up" and ready to spring into action, a feeling similar to a sprinter in the starting block. In my classes, I am constantly confronted with students who are very reluctant to assume the correct posture because they are convinced that it is unnatural. Let me give you the additional explanation I give them:

Pretend you want to catch a golf bag with all the golf clubs inside. Instinctively, what kind of posture would you assume? Certainly not one with a straight back and arms stretched out. You could catch something light that way, but your arms, which would have to carry the whole load by themselves in this position, would not be able to hold anything heavy. Without giving it much thought, your body would automatically bend slightly forward with the upper arms close to the body. And this is exactly the posture you want to assume in golf. This athletic posture is necessary in order to move your body correctly during the swing.

You can't catch a heavy object by simply extending your arms (left); but assume an athletic posture and you don't encounter problems.

43

Arms, Hands, and the Club

In the correct posture, you position your arms comfortably next to your body. Your upper arms are in contact with your body halfway to your elbows. You should

The posture is the same regardless of what club you use, because the distance between the end of the handle vertically to the ground is the same for all golf clubs.

stand with about the width of your fist between your thighs and hands. Once you have assumed this posture, with the clubhead resting on the ground and the weight of your body evenly balanced between the heels and the balls of the feet, the distance between your feet is also correct. Another point to keep in mind: in the correct posture, the lower arms and the club will form an angle (viewed from the side). The shorter the club, the larger the angle, because of the lie, which also requires an increased flexion of the wrists towards the side of the small finger. Aside

This is the side view of the correct posture.

from this detail, the posture assumed for taking a full swing is the same no matter what kind of golf club you use, because the distance between the end of the handle and the ground is the same, regardless of the length of the shaft.

Position of the Head

The head should be a straight extension of the spine. Many players have a tendency to lower their heads too far, thinking that they are getting a better view of the ball. However, it is better to look at the ball with the nose raised a bit, because when the body begins to rotate, the left shoulder should fit under the chin without moving on a plane that is too steep. Players who constantly need to be reminded to keep their heads still and "down" during the swing develop a much greater tendency to bury their heads in their chests as soon as they are in the approach position. It is almost impossible to swing a golf club properly in such a position. A player has to hold his head straight, not tilted to the side. Tilting the head negatively influences a player's sense of balance and interferes with the initial starting position of the club.

The Stance

When using a medium iron, a golfer stands with the equivalent of the width of his shoulders between his feet. Both hands are slightly to the left of the vertical midline of the body.

Width of the Stance

The stance is the distance between both feet when standing on the ground. The golfer must find a good compromise between the ability to rotate the body and still stand solidly on the ground. The greater the distance between the feet, the more stable the stance, but the more difficult it will be to rotate the body. The ideal stance for most golfers is with the width of their shoulders between their feet. The shinbones, or the middle of the feet, are vertically in line with the outside of the shoulders. Athletic golfers usually stand with their feet a little farther apart; those who are not quite as flexible, stand with their feet somewhat closer together. These are the recommendations when using a medium-long club (a 5 or 7 iron); when using longer clubs, the stance is a little wider; and with shorter clubs, the feet are somewhat closer together.

Feet and Knees

The golfer rotates his left foot about 25 degrees to the outside. This makes rotating the lower part of body to the outside easier. The right foot is almost straight in line with the target and only slightly turned to the outside. The lower half of the body rotates less during the backswing than during the downswing, and the foot in this position provides better resistance than a foot rotated farther to the outside. The exact same situation prevails when a baseball is hit: the back leg is vertical to the direction of the hit. The knees are almost vertical

to the legs (viewed from the front).

Distribution of Weight

Since the right hand is below the left on the handle of the club and, therefore, is somewhat more forward, the right shoulder is also lower than the left. This results in the upper body leaning slightly to the right. If you were to place a golfer in this position on two scales (one foot on one scale and the other foot on the second), you would probably see the weight distributed as 51 percent on the right side and 49 percent on the left. This difference is hardly noticeable.

Players who seem to have a problem during the backswing always try to compensate for it by shifting their weight heavily to the right foot in the address position. We strongly disapprove of such a practice because while the weight shifted to the right foot is insignificant, the player's balance changes.

In the section on posture, we discussed distributing the player's weight between the heels and the balls of the feet. Although the player wants to distribute his weight evenly between the heels and the balls of the feet, he can shift the emphasis somewhat more to the balls of the feet.

POSTURE AND STANCE

Position of the Ball

The position of the ball depends on the length of the golf club. The reason is obvious: with a short iron, a player cares more about precision than about distance.

You achieve precision with a strong backspin on the ball, which provides stability and height and limits the distance the ball rolls. In turn, you can increase the backspin when you hit the ball with a steep angle of attack: the closer the ball is to the right foot, the steeper the angle of attack. When using a short iron (a sand wedge or 8 iron), place the ball in the center of the stance.

Usually, players use a wood for hitting long balls when they don't want a strong backspin, because the ball will travel on a flat curve and roll as far as possible after hitting the ground. Likewise, a steep angle of attack shortens the distance of the hit because the force of the clubhead is not fully in the direction of the target. Therefore, when using a wood, place the ball almost vertically (slightly to the right) in line and on the inside of the left heel. The result is that the clubhead hits the ball at approximately the lowest point (vertex) of the arc of the swing.

When using a long or a medium iron, the ideal position of the ball is between these two points.

Some critics insist on always putting the ball in the same place, arguing that the vertical angle of attack changes sufficiently with different clubs simply because the plane in which the arms travel is steeper or flatter, depending on the club. In order to understand that this influence is actually rather minimal and, therefore, not sufficient, hold a flat disk (a record or a CD) at an angle of about 55 degrees, corresponding to the lie of a wood, in front of you. Change to an angle of approximately 65 degrees, corresponding to the lie of a wedge. At the lowest point (viewed from the front), the arc changes so little that it is clear that you have to take other actions in order to hit the ball easily, either with a wood from a tee when swinging back or with a wedge when swinging down (divot).

When using a short iron, place the ball in the middle of the stance; when using a wood, place it slightly towards the left heel; when using a medium or long iron, place the ball between these two points.

POSTURE AND STANCE

If you place the ball too far to the left, your shoulders will point to the left of the target, causing a slice or pull.

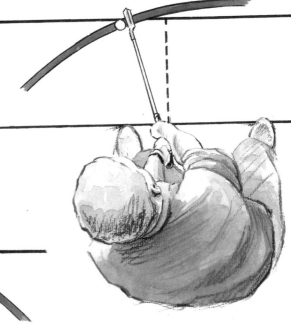

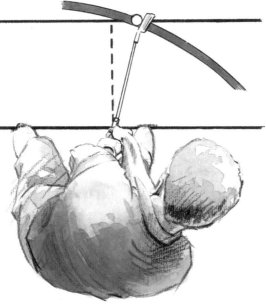

If you place the ball too far to the right, the shoulders point to the right of the target, causing a hook or push.

The position of the ball is also important because it influences the position of the shoulders. For instance, if you place the ball too far to the left, your shoulders are also pointing to the left of the target. It is almost impossible to guide the club back to the proper direction. Of course, the same holds true if you place the ball too far to the right. The shoulders are then pointing to the right of the target, and the plane of the clubface usually tilts to the right also.

Position of the Hands and the Ball

Often golf instructors advise students to hold their left arms and the club (viewed from the front) in a straight line so that, at the moment of impact, the hands are in front of the ball. I believe that such a position is rather dangerous because during the first part of the swing the player pulls the club back too flat. My experience is that the position of the hands in the address position has minimal impact. Hand position should primarily guarantee a correct backswing.

The player can easily find the proper position for his hands by taking a wood, placing the ball (as discussed) in the vicinity of the left heel, and assuming the proper position for the hands: the club will be vertical to the ground (viewed from the front).

The position is the same regardless of what kind of club the player uses and regardless of where the player places the ball, which means (viewed from the target) that the hands are in front of the ball when using a short iron, at the same height when using a medium or long iron, and slightly behind the ball when using a wood. To check your hand position, place a tee in the hole at the end of the handle. This must point to the left half of the body.

Posture and Stance

▶ To make yourself shorter, you have to bend forward while keeping your back straight.

▶ When viewed from the side, the shoulders are vertically in line with both knees and both heels.

▶ The chin is high, and the head is straight, not tilted to either side.

▶ The feet are the width of the shoulders apart; the left foot points slightly to the outside; and the right foot points straight ahead.

▶ Depending on the club, the ball is in the middle of the stance (short iron) and slightly to the right on the inside of the left heel (wood and tee).

▶ In the address position, the hands are slightly to the left of the center of the body.

PRE-SHOT ROUTINE

Locating the target, aiming, using a trigger, and addressing the ball should be part of every golfer's pre-shot routine.

In golf, it is easy to see the difference between a beginner and an experienced player just by observing the way that they look at a target. While the beginner concentrates almost exclusively on the ball, the experienced player spends much of his time and effort evaluating his target because he knows that even if his swing is perfect, the ball might never reach the target if the club and his body are pointing in the wrong direction. We'll explain why this is so difficult in the following chapter.

Locating the Target

Even before a golfer pulls a club out of the bag, he should be absolutely clear what his target is. Most amateurs have only a fuzzy idea where they want to hit the ball, even when they are in the address position. In addition, the flag and the target are often thought to be the same. But under most circumstances, this is wrong. When teeing off or hitting a long shot, situations in which you cannot reach the flag in one attempt, and particularly when hitting out of the rough, the surest way is seldom the direct one.

The same, of course, holds true on the practice range. To my question "Where are you aiming," the most common answer is "Straight ahead." But "straight ahead" does not define an actual target because a ball can fly straight in many different directions. In order to define a straight line, you need two reference points: a ball and a sign indicating distance to the target or a flag. Without these reference points, you cannot determine if you have been successful in reaching the intended target.

The first order of business on the golf course, as well as the range, should always be to establish a precise target that your ball is to reach.

Before attempting a shot, a player must accurately determine the location of the target. Only in rare instances will the target be the flag.

Aiming

In golf, aiming is particularly problematic because the player stands parallel to the line between the ball and the target and not in front of it. This means that his line of view is somewhat offset and a considerable distance from the direct line between the ball and the target. In other sports where a specific object is to be moved to a target (archery, bowling, billiards, etc.), one of the player's eyes is always either in line or directly above the line to the target.

The problem to be solved by the golfer is to line his body up parallel to the target line, pointing from the ball to the target. In order to do this, he would have to turn his head 90 degrees, to aim at a specific point as far from the target as his feet are from the ball, and, last but not least, to place his feet on this imaginary line that runs parallel to the target line.

To accomplish this with 100 percent accuracy is almost impossible. For instance, if a player placed one foot only 2 inches (5 cm) too far forward or back, he would be, assuming his stance is 18 inches (50 cm), off his target by 16 yards (15 m) if the distance to the target is 165 yards (150 m).

PRE-SHOT ROUTINE

On the golf course, stand in this position to search for an intermediate target that should be no more than 1 yard (91 cm) away.

Therefore, from a lateral prospective, it is impossible for a golfer to align himself properly. In addition, when aiming at a target, almost every golfer reacts to the result of his previous shot. Players who are constantly hitting the ball to the left always try to compensate by aiming more to the right. Eventually, they believe they are hitting straight. Following is a discussion about aiming correctly.

After a test swing, the golfer moves (viewed from the target) behind the ball. From this position, he finds a so-called intermediate target, which should be anywhere between 8–40 inches (20–100 cm) from the ball and directly in line with the target line. The intermediate target might be an old divot, a blade of grass, or any other natural object on the turf. After the player has decided on his intermediate target, he takes his club and places the clubhead directly behind the ball so that the clubface is squarely pointing to the intermediate target. The explanation for this is relatively simple: a player will find it much easier to aim the club at a point that is, at most, 1 yard (91 cm) away than at one that is 165 yards (150 m) away.

In order to shorten this rather time-consuming procedure, a player on the practice

range can place a club in front of his feet so that it is parallel to the target line. On the golf course, however, a player has no excuse not to precede as outlined above, unless he does not care about the outcome.

To practise, place a club on the ground in front of your feet and line it up parallel to the target line.

PRE-SHOT ROUTINE

Adjustments

*First, orient the
face of the club
towards the
intermediate
target . . .*

*. . . then posi-
tion the body so
that it forms a
right angle with
the leading
edge.*

The player puts the clubface
in position at the same time
as he places his right foot so
that it is vertical to the target
line. Then, he immediately
looks beyond the intermediate
target directly to the real target. In this position, the player's body is slightly to the left
of the target. The next step is
to put the left foot into the
final position and to correct
the position of the right foot
to establish the proper stance.
The player's body is now
properly facing the target
line. This means that shoulders, hips, knees, feet, and
the lower arms are all parallel
to the target line. Now, the
player will look one more
time towards the target. During this phase, many beginners feel a tension in their
bodies. The experienced
player, however, is very relaxed. Some players move
their feet rhythmically, like
tennis players waiting for op-
ponents to serve. Others
move the club up and down
or do a so-called waggle. The
latter is a movement of the
lower arms and wrists which
causes the club to swing back
and forth aboveground. If a
player's hands and forearms
are tense, the club will make
jerky movements instead.

The imaginary line through the shoulders, lower arms, hips, knees, and feet must run parallel to the intended line to the target.

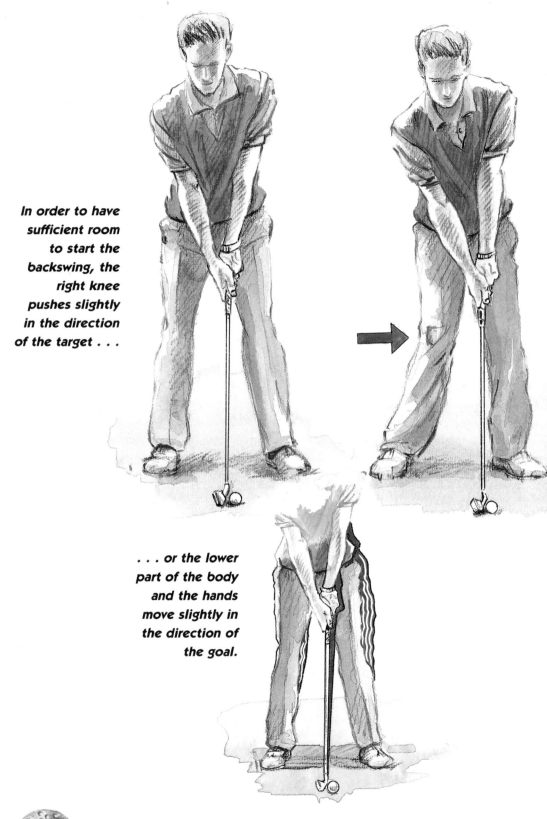

In order to have sufficient room to start the backswing, the right knee pushes slightly in the direction of the target . . .

. . . or the lower part of the body and the hands move slightly in the direction of the goal.

Trigger

Another problem golfers face is having to go immediately from a quiet address position to a flowing rhythmical movement. In other sports that also use a ball (tennis, soccer basketball, etc.), the player is already in motion before making contact with the ball. To make this transition a little easier, many golfers initiate their swing with a so-called trigger. This trigger can be any kind of movement that the player does before beginning the backswing. Some players push their right knee in the direction of the target before they begin (for example, Roger Davis); other players first move the club up and down. Their trigger is the act of putting the club on the ground (for example, Nick Faldo). A forward-press trigger involves moving the hands slightly in the direction of the target before starting the backswing. Players should only use this trigger if they are able to bring the clubhead back to the previously established position.

As you can see, the ball sits motionless on the ground, and this is not necessarily an advantage. This position definitely creates problems, not the least of which are mental. The player has a lot time to think about all the things that can go wrong long before he hits the ball. The goal, then, should be to establish a very precise sequence of actions —grip, test swing, aiming, adjustments, and trigger— before hitting the ball, so that

Pre-shot Routine

▶ Establish a clear target on the practice range and on the golf course.
▶ Stand behind the ball and find an intermediate target about 1 yard (91 cm) in front of the ball.
▶ Next, point the clubface towards the intermediate target and then line up the whole body vertically to the leading edge.
▶ Decide on a trigger so that the backswing has a "flying start."
▶ Use this pre-shot routine consistently, every time you get ready to swing. This is the best assurance that each swing will be consistent, producing the same results as often as possible and reducing the amount of time spent worrying about possible errors.

the swing which follows these movements will always be the same. In addition, a specific sequence does not allow time to think about the consequences of a possible error. A player who prepares differently before each hit must also be prepared for a different swing each time.

THE SWING

The goal of the swing is to consistently bring the clubface and the sweet spot to the ball at high speed while swinging in the direction of the target.

The player goes through four basic movements during the course of the swing. These movements allow the club to travel on the proper plane.

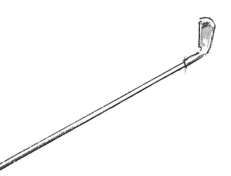

Four Basic Movements

Now you know the most important steps to take before every golf swing (grip, posture, stance, and pre-shot routine). They are the most difficult parts of learning the game of golf. What is left is swinging the club in the proper plane while generating enough speed to produce the necessary energy. For that to take place, the player has to go through four basic movements.

Rotating the Body

In the address position, the body must rotate around the spine. The backswing produces muscular tension between the upper and lower parts of the body because the upper body is wound up about twice as far (90 degrees) as the lower part (45 degrees). In the following explanations, I will refer to the shoulder rotation in relation to the changes in the address position. To determine the actual rotation of the shoulders, always deduct the degree of rotation of the lower part of the body.

The body releases the energy created during the backswing during the downswing. This energy is the prerequisite for the speed of the clubhead.

Since the body only rotates in the address position, no vertical movements (high or low) take place during the swing. The shoulders, therefore, move on a relatively flat plane and vertical to the forward angle of the upper body. (In the address position, this is 30 degrees.) Every part of the body that is in front of the spine, which serves as an axis, moves to the right during the backswing and to the left in the downswing.

THE SWING

Flexing the Wrists

During the backswing, the wrists flex in the direction of the side of the thumb (radial flexion). During the downswing, they flex towards the side of the little finger (ulnar flexion). During a golf swing, the wrists create a two-lever system that multiplies the energy created by the movements of the body and arms. A proper grip (see page 20) is essential for good wrist action.

Rotating the Arms

The lower arms rotate clockwise during the backswing (pronation of the lower left arm, supination of the lower right arm); rotation during the downswing is the reverse. These rotating actions guarantee that the club always remains in the same plane during the swing.

Moving Arms Away from the Body

During the backswing, the arms move up and away from the body. At the highest point of the backswing, the left arm (viewed from the side) is at the same level as the shaft at the address position. The distance between the upper arms and the body should primarily increase during the second half of the backswing so that the arms lift into the proper plane. The level of this plane corresponds to that of the lie of the club used: between 55 degrees and 63 degrees. The plane is steeper than the one in which the shoulders move. This corresponds to lifting the arms away from the body during the backswing and moving them back down during the downswing as the upper body rotates back.

The player must make sure that the club is travelling on the right plane and that the arms move on a steeper plane than the rotating shoulders.

Many players use more than the four basic movements. This is not necessary. While these players are able to produce good, solid hits, they are seldom able to do so with any consistency. We believe that adding to the basic movements leads to compensating movements, making the golf swing unnecessarily complicated. And in the final analysis, consistency is what every golfer aims for. Almost every player can hit a golf ball successfully now and then, but few players can do so on a regular basis. Thus, a player ought not to think that, generally speaking, his swing is correct just because he is successful once in a while. Those "good" hits are often a result of good luck and coincidence in which the

mistakes the player makes cancel each other out. In addition, it is wrong to assume that only a bad swing has to be corrected in order to improve. When a player properly analyzes videos, it becomes clear that all his swings look the same, assuming that the video wasn't taken while the golfer was changing his swing. A ball that reacts differently in the course of several attempts is an indication that the same error might have different effects.

The notion that a player's practice swings are perfect and things only go wrong when he adds a ball to the equation is just as mistaken. With practice swings, we can never be sure if the clubhead has returned to the exact same position in the address position or if the ball would have been hit with the sweet spot. We know just as little about the position of the clubface at the moment of impact. Both factors decisively influence the flight of the ball, and yet they might be totally incorrect during the practice swing without the player being aware of it—which then, of course, leads to the wrong conclusions.

Obviously, Bernhard Langer uses the four basic movements to bring the clubhead to the ball correctly.

THE SWING

The Planes

In discussing golf techniques, the most important and most misunderstood term is "the plane." Although different parts of the body move on

This drawing shows the planes on which the club, the arms, and the shoulders travel.

different planes, the three most important are: the club, arm, and shoulder planes.

We'll discuss all three planes in more detail later. However, here I would like to give you a quick overview.

Club Plane

One of the most important principles in golf is: *The shaft of the club should always move in the same plane that it assumed during the address position. If the shaft is parallel to the ground, it must also be parallel to the target line.*

This means that if you stop at any time during the swing, the shaft should (viewed from the side) remain at the same angle to the ground as the lie of the club.

If the club is parallel to the ground (as is the case in the backswing when the club has travelled 90 degrees or when the club is 90 degrees in front of the ball during the down-swing), it must also be parallel to the target line, meaning that it is pointing slightly to the left of the target.

A club that travels consistently on the same plane has the best chance of returning to the same place where it was in the address position. If, on the other hand, the plane is too flat (shaft of the club positioned too far horizontally) the club will usually

From the start through the moment of impact, the club moves on the exact same plane.

The shaft of the club always remains parallel to the plane.

At the highest point of the backswing, the arms are parallel to the plane.

THE SWING

swing too far to the outside and hit the ball with the heel. In addition, the club will also travel too far down. In other words, it won't gain enough ground. Finally, when the club is swinging on a plane that is too flat, the lower arms will rotate too much, usually closing the clubface when it reaches the ball (tilted to the right).

Correspondingly, when the club plane is too steep (the shaft of the club is too vertical), the tip almost always hits the ball, and the divots are too deep. In addition, the forearms usually rotate too little, and the clubface is too open when it reaches the ball (tilted to the right). The central theme of the golf swing is the plane the club travels on. Here is where we find most of the problems that cause errors. Mark O'Meara and Chip Beck are two examples of golfers who have perfected their club plane.

Arm Plane

We usually discuss the arm plane in connection with the highest point of the backswing. What is meant here is the angle of the left arm (the connecting line between the end of the handle and the left shoulder), as viewed from the side. Ideally, this plane corresponds to the original plane of the club, in other words, to the lie of the club, and depends on the club the player is using. The longer the shaft (meaning the less lie), the flatter the plane of the arm. In this context, I also always pay attention to the "road" the arm travels on its way to the highest point. Since the hands, or more precisely the end of the handle, hardly move down during the swing from where they are in the address position, they travel upwards in a steep and slightly concave curve.

Shoulder Plane

In contrast to the arm plane, the shoulder plane is much flatter. The forward bend of the upper body in the address position determines the shoulder plane. Ideally, the shoulders rotate on a plane that is exactly vertical to the angle of the upper body. If the plane at the highest point is too flat, the player has straightened his upper body too much during the backswing. If, on the other hand, the plane is too steep (tilted shoulders), that is a sign that the player has tried to make himself shorter. Since the position of the arms and, therefore, the club change whenever the position of the spine changes, the player needs to pay a lot of attention to posture during

The hands pri-
marily move up,
and the left
shoulder rotates
to the right.

the swing in order to assure the best possible results.

In order to describe the four basic movements chronologically and in detail, I have divided the golf swing into ten stages. (The photos do not show a single swing.)

Remember that these photos only convey snapshots of a whole movement. However, a golf swing does not consist of a number of individual positions, but rather of one fluid motion. After analyzing and then correcting specific parts of a movement, a player must integrate the changes he makes back into a whole movement.

This chapter isn't a list from which a player checks off point after point. Rather, a player should think of it more as a dictionary in which he can find answers to very specific question that seem to crop up time and again during the learning process.

Even if the amount of information that follows seems intimidating, remember that you can ignore all those things that you are already doing well. However, if you detect a mistake, you must find the corresponding movement that needs to be changed. After you correct the mistakes and practise the new movements sufficiently, you must integrate them so that they become automatic as quickly as possible.

The Backswing

In order to determine the original angle of the club, we have included another photo of the address position. The line extended past the handle of the club represents the plane of the club (viewed from the side). The lie of the club (here a 6 iron) determines the angle; the longer the club, the flatter the plane and vice versa.

The address position viewed from the side: the length of the club determines the plane.

The address position viewed from the front.

Phase 1

After going through the trigger movements, pull the club back so that (viewed from the side) it remains in its plane. Move your hands, arms, shoulders, and to a slight degree your hips, so that your arms and the club form a Y, allowing the spine to rotate as an axis. Continue this movement until the club has covered over 45 degrees. Up to this point, you only use active force during the side movement; the club will move up and down automatically with the momentum created by the rotation of the spine.

Preparing for a swing always feels unnatural if the player tries to do either of the following: pull the club back by moving either up or flat across the ground or pull back by moving the club too far to the inside or back directly over the target line. You know that your swing is correct when you have the feeling that no individual part of your body is moving independently of the others.

To determine if the Y remained unchanged during this phase, check to see if the end of the handle and the front edge of the clubhead (the leading edge) are still pointing to the left side of the body; also, the distance between the end of the handle and this point should change very little, if at all.

Up to the point where the club has covered about 90 degrees, the head of the club must point directly to the target line. Providing that the end of the handle has moved

Whenever the club is parallel to the ground, it must also be parallel to the target line.

only to the right, this guarantees that the club always remains on the same plane. Surprisingly enough, most golf teachers immediately correct a player when he pulls the club too far to the outside (angle too steep). At the same time, most teachers totally ignore the same movement in the opposite direction: too much to the inside (angle too flat).

Phase 2

In this phase, the lower arms and the wrists begin to move. The wrists begin to flex, and the lower arms begin to rotate. Wrist flexion moves the club up, and the rotation of the lower arm moves the club back. However, remember that moving the club back is secondary to the upward movement, so that the club can reach the highest point of the arc. Therefore, flexing the hand is much more obvious than the rotation of the lower arms. To make sure that you carry out both actions equally and properly, your club, when parallel to the ground, must also be parallel to the target line. If that is the case, and if the edge of the left hand is vertical above the outside of the left foot, you have

75

THE SWING

correctly carried out both basic movements: flexing the wrists and rotating the lower arms. Up to this point, the end of the handle has only moved to the right.

If the shaft points to the right of the goal at the moment when it is parallel to the ground, you have either flexed your wrists too late or rotated your lower arms too much (for example, Barry Lane, Bernhard Langer, and Raymond Floyd). On the other hand, if the rotation of the lower arms was insufficient and the wrists flexed too early, the shaft points to the left of the goal (for example, Ronan Rafferty and Johnny Miller).

Another small tip for those who have noticed that they are pulling the golf club on too flat a plane: Do not try to hold the club farther away from your body at the beginning of the swing by moving your arms to the outside (away from the body); this only moves the end of the handle forward instead to the right.

If, as we suggested, you move the club back, and the angle between the lower left arm and the wrists does not change, the leading edge will not point in the air (as others often suggest), but will line up parallel to the left lower arm. This means that the lower edge of the clubface has rotated slightly counterclockwise compared to the vertical position (from the golfer's point of view). Throughout the swing (except in the phase just before and after the moment of impact), the leading edge remains parallel to the left lower arm. In the second phase, the body is also a little more wound up.

Phase 3
In this phase, the club travels an additional 90 degrees and (viewed from the front) assumes a vertical position to the ground. The golfer continues to build on the actions necessary for the basic movements:

▶ The hands (viewed from the side) move in the direction of and towards the highest point in the swing. For this to happen, the player must move his arms away from his body. The following example should help to demonstrate the action:

A player in the address position holds one towel under each arm. He should not allow the towels to fall to the ground between the address position and Phase 3. When he moves the club upwards, the arms have to move away from the body, and the tow-

▶ The greatest change during this phase (viewed from the front) is in the angle between the lower arms and the shaft of the club. This angle is approximately 90 degrees, which means that in this phase you strongly flex the wrists to the side of the thumb. The advantage of flexing the wrists early is that this action does not have to take place during the critical phase of the swing (just before the change in direction to the inside). Although flexion is still possible during that moment, it requires much more effort and coordination to do it in a controlled manner (as, for example, Jack Nicklaus and Curtis Strange do).

Flexing the wrists early also acknowledges the fact that the club must move high into the air but only a little to the rear. If a golfer flexes his wrists too late, the club will have completed (after having passed 90 degrees) most of the back movement but very little of the upward movement. But do not start flexing too early because that would turn the clubhead too far to the outside. Let the wrists remain passive during the first part of the swing. This guarantees a controlled return to the plane that the club is to travel on.

Although positioned slightly above the original plane, the club always remains parallel to it.

At this point, the player has flexed his wrists enough so that the shaft of the club and his left arm form a right angle.

els fall down. If the towels do not fall, the swing is too flat.

The same happens in stick ball: in the windup, the throwing arm moves away from the body, returning to the body during the forward movement.

With the flexion of the wrists, the right elbow also starts to bend slightly.

▶ The lower arms continue to rotate with the shaft of the club remaining at the original level. If the angle is too steep, you have not rotated the lower arms enough; if the angle is too flat, you rotated them too much. Since the end of the handle is now above the original plane, the end of the handle will point slightly to the outside of the target line.

▶ Aside from a minimal amount of rotation (compared to the address position, the shoulders have only turned about 70 degrees), the body posture has not changed much during this phase.

We have already covered three of the four basic movements of the backswing: moving the arms away from the body, rotating the lower arms, and the radial flexion of the wrists.

Phase 4
The rotation of the body during the last part of the backswing plays the most important role. Since the club, hands, and arms are already in their proper rela-

tionship to the body, the player only needs to concentrate on bringing them into the right position by rotating his body correctly.

The body rotates until the shoulders are at a right angle to the target line: the hips will then have turned 35–45 degrees. This rotation movement and the rotation of the shoulders build tension in the body that increases unless the player turns his hips. Inexperienced players often try

The plane of the shaft is identical to what it was in the address position.

78

A club swing that has gone through 270 degrees must be parallel to the target line; the left arm is parallel to the plane of the club (left).

The shoulders have rotated 90 degrees (right).

to avoid this necessary accumulation of tension in the body. They either rotate their shoulders too little or their hips too much. The latter is the case when the player's left foot comes too far off the ground.

Older, less flexible players often have difficulty rotating their shoulders 90 degrees when they only rotate their hips 45 degrees. The main problem this creates is that at the highest point in the backswing, the club does not point in the direction of the target but rather too far to the left of it. This increases the player's tendency to slice the ball, reducing the distance the ball will travel even more. One way of dealing with this problem is to allow the hips to follow the

rotation of the shoulders a bit more than recommended. Of course, this will reduce the degree of tension between the upper and lower body and, therefore, the speed of the clubhead, but at least the player will hit the ball straighter than would otherwise be the case. In other words, the reason for a short hit is not a lack of power but a lack of flexibility on the part of the player.

THE SWING

Lateral Movement

With the body completely wound up, the player's head is now half the width of his head to the right. Most golfers have a hard time picturing themselves rotating around their spines, the center of their bodies. The following explanation might make it easier to picture this:

Instead of one axis (representing the center of the body and, therefore, precluding any movement of the head to either side), picture the body as having two (a backswing axis and a follow-through axis), both located in the hips. During the backswing, the body rotates around the right axis, and during the follow-through, around the left. If the player moves outside these, any lateral movement will be too strong.

However, during the backswing, the player must make sure that only the upper body moves sideways. The lower body, particularly the right leg, should not move to the right. Rather, the right leg supports the upper body. The tension that has been building up in the muscles in the back of the right thigh during the backswing releases during the downswing.

Distance Covered During Backswing

Much as the approach run in the pole vault, golf also has an optimum approach movement. In pole vaulting, the force at the moment of the jump does not necessarily give the jumper more height. For instance, it makes no difference in pole vaulting if you increase the approach run by 100 yards (92 m). The same is true in golf: the speed of the club does not increase if you swing the club as far back as possible. The ideal length of the backswing, however, is different for each golfer. The most important points are that the upper body rotates sufficiently and that the wrists flex completely. How far the arms swing back is far less important. For most golfers, the backswing travels back much too far most of the time. Usually, the reason is that the club does not move on the proper plane, so it takes longer to get the club back into the proper plane for the downswing. In most cases, the angle of the arms is then also too steep. Another reason might be that the wrists flex too late and the arm movement and the body's rotation

The club always moves in the same plane, as determined by the lie of the club.

THE SWING

finish before the club can start on the downswing, because the angle between the left lower arm and the shaft is not yet large enough. In both cases, the club moves too far back during the backswing. The average backswing with a wood reaches its highest point when the club moves just past the 270 degree point. When the club is shorter, the backswing is also shorter; a full swing with a wedge covers about 225 degrees.

Many golfers believe that they can solve their swing problems by either slowing down or shortening their backswing. Of course, this would simplify the swing and allow them to compensate for possible errors in movement. However, the goal should always be to learn the proper sequence of movements; speed and the length of the movements are rather secondary.

Left Arm

Much discussion takes place about the position of the left arm during the backswing. But, as we have already mentioned, in the approach position the play relaxes this arm and extends it alongside the body. The arm remains in this position, even during the swing. The player neither shortens it nor lengthens it during the backswing because

either attempt would require a compensating movement. The player should not try to stiffen the arm in order to avoid lengthening it. It is less tragic for the elbow to bend slightly during the backswing than for the arm to lengthen unnaturally, because the centrifugal force during the downswing stretches the arm naturally. Actually, during the downswing, the club pulls the arms down with a force that is equal to 100 pounds (45 kg).

Other Influences on the High Point of the Backswing

Additional details influence the swing when the club reaches the end point of the backswing. Golf teachers often mention these when discussing the swing because they can analyze them on a video tape. The following require the player's attention:

▶ The player has to maintain the proper angle position between hips and knees that we spoke of in the address position. Since the rotation of the body in the approach position has created tension in the body, many golfers tend to avoid this tension by trying to make themselves taller. However, this requires a compensating movement that makes repetition difficult.

► The hands and both elbows form an equidistant triangle. The left arm is parallel to the plane of the club. The lower right arm is parallel to the spine, and the upper right arm is almost parallel to the ground. The elbow is somewhat below the right shoulder.

The angle between the upper right arm and the shoulders is approximately 135 degrees, but no more than that, because a larger angle would cause the arms to move too far away from the body (for example, Fred Couples).

► The end of the handle of a wood is visible between the hands and the head (viewed from the side) and should also be parallel to the ground and the target line. If a club, for example an iron, does not reach 270 degrees, then the shaft must point farther left to the target in order to reach the proper plane. (Here, too, the club remains parallel to its original plane). The front, lower edge of the clubhead (the leading edge) is still parallel to that of the lower left arm. If in this position the clubface points into the air, the player has closed it too much (rotated it to the left). If it is pointing forward, the player has opened it too much (rotated it to the right). In

both cases, the player must check the grip, the flexion of the wrists (pointing in the direction of the back of the hands or the inside of the hands, respectively), and the plane of the arm; because most of the time, the reason for a tilted clubface position involves one of these.

► The shoulders and the spine form a right angle. This means that during the backswing, the left shoulder moves down automatically and the right shoulder moves up automatically. One mistake players frequently make is tilting their shoulders (for example, Steven Richardson). When this happens, they have usually dropped their left shoulder too far down during the backswing. Players who have a tendency to do this should not concentrate on turning their left shoulders below the chins because this causes dipping. Instead, they should move their left shoulders to the right (or behind the ball). The shoulder moves down automatically because the upper body is bending forward.

When a player dips his shoulder, he often bends his upper body too far forward in the address position, or he swings the club back too far or too closed in, trying to

THE SWING

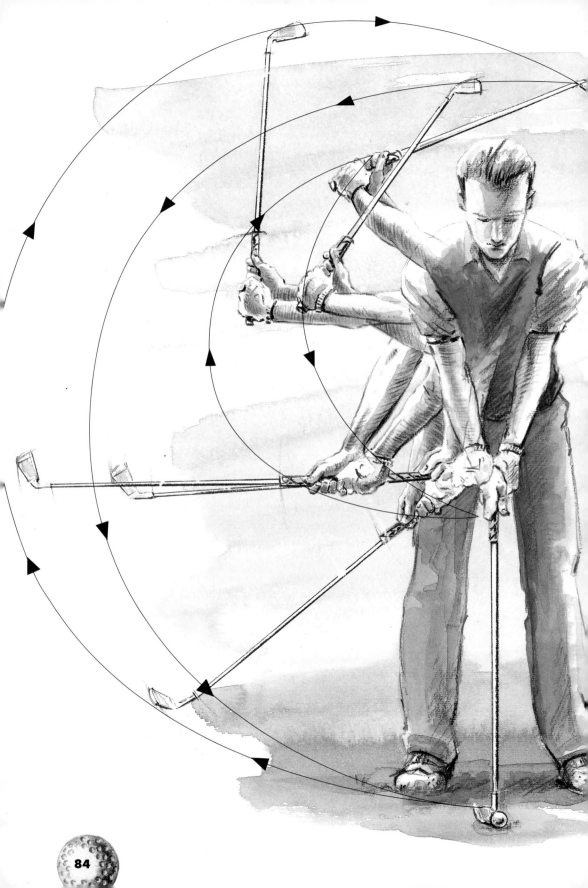

move the club into a straight line. If the position of the arms and shoulders is correct, the plane of the arms is somewhat steeper than that of the shoulders.

The clubhead and hands move in a larger curve during the backswing than during the downswing.

▶ Contrary to what many golfers believe, what the heel of the left shoe does is much less important than other factors. Whether or not the heel lifts off the ground depends on the length of the club used and on the flexibility of the player. If the player is very flexible or the backswing is short, the heel can remain on the ground. However, it is not a mistake if the heel lifts slightly off the ground. But the player needs to be sure that his left knee does not just flip to the right, which would be the case if the lower half of the body moves incorrectly (moving to the left during the backswing).

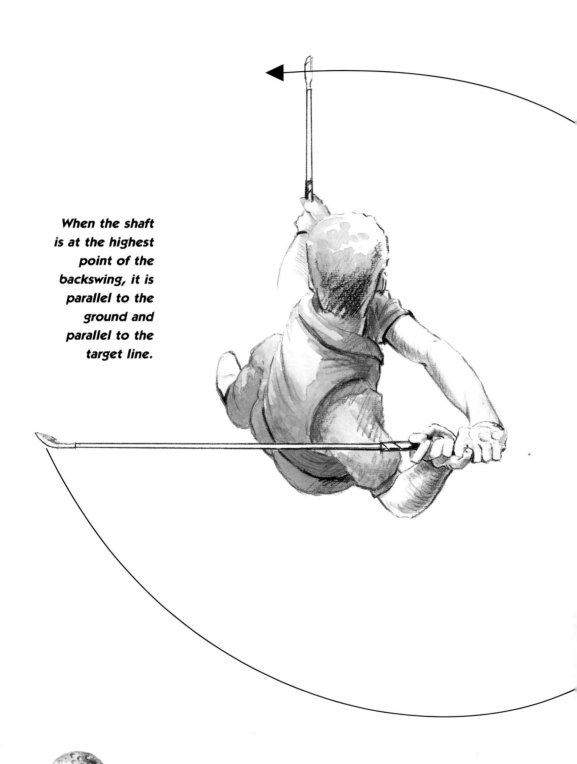

When the shaft is at the highest point of the backswing, it is parallel to the ground and parallel to the target line.

The Downswing

The downswing begins at the highest point of the backswing and ends at the moment of impact. This is the most important part of the golf swing because it includes actual contact with the ball. No matter how unorthodox your backswing, if your clubface consistently hits the ball correctly, you will never encounter problems with your long hits. Of course, I don't want to minimize the importance of the backswing, because the better the backswing, the fewer compensating movements you have to make during the downswing.

The downswing is particularly difficult to steer because it lasts all of 0.2 seconds. The first thing a player needs to know is that the downswing is not the symmetrical reverse of the backswing. In fact, the situation at the moment of impact is totally different from the one in the address position, and the sequence of the individual movements is also markedly different.

In addition, the backswing and the downswing are not two totally separate movements, since, just as in throwing a baseball, you don't pause between the two. (In reality, for just a moment, the club is still moving back while the lower half of the body has already begun to turn towards the goal.)

You apply the same four fundamental elements of the backswing to the downswing, except in reverse order. However, when you release the wrist flexion and the lower-arm rotation, centrifugal force creates additional momentum.

The remaining movements, rotating the body rotation and pulling the arms back to the body, initiate the downswing. During the backswing, the lower body follows the movements of the upper body; during the downswing, the upper body follows the lower body.

The shaft is parallel to the original plane of the club and, just as in the backswing, slightly above it (left).

Phase 5

The downswing starts with simultaneous movements of the left knee, the left hip, and the arms. The left knee and the left hip move to the left in the direction of the target, while the hands are moving down in the direction of the position that is necessary at the moment of impact. Immediately after these lateral movements, the lower body begins to rotate. In turn, this leads the upper body to rotate back also. The shoulders don't catch up with the hips until after the moment of impact. The upper body dips slightly to the right during the downswing, causing the right shoulder to be slightly lower than the left shoulder when compared to its position during the backswing.

The downward movement of the hands, which is automatic because of the centrifugal force, brings the arms closer to the body. This is the reverse of the movement away from the body that takes place during the backswing.

Be sure that the distance between the hands and the right shoulder increases steadily. In the case of almost every golfer whose balls start out to the left and then turn to the right, this increase is much too slow during the first part of the downswing.

During the first phase of the downswing, the sluggishness of the clubhead, which is the heaviest part of the golf club, ensures that the angle between the left arm and the club (viewed from the front) becomes smaller. You can observe this action when watching the golf swing of all the top players.

During the downswing, the distance between the right shoulder and the hands must increase steadily (right).

89

During the downswing, the arms swing down and the hips move out of the way by rotating sideways to the left.

Average golfers, especially those dealing with slicing problems, cannot implement what we outlined above because the timely dissolution of the angle between the lower left arm and the clubhead from this position requires an enormous amount of power and coordination.

On one hand, the art of the downswing consists of coordinating the movements of the body and, on the other hand, coordinating the movement of the arms, hands, and the club.

A strong player is much more likely to have difficulty fighting quick hand and arm movements that often close the face of the club too early and cause the ball to veer off to the left. The hands of the weaker player usually cannot follow the quicker movement of the body, particularly that of the upper body. The face of the club is then open at the moment of impact, causing the ball to veer too far to the right. Such a player should never slow down or delay at the moment of impact (opening the angle between the club and the arms).

During this phase, the right elbow is considerably lower than the left. Again, the club is parallel to its original plane. The golfer needs to be in this position for the club to reach the ball at the moment of impact from the inside rather than from outside of the target line, which always happens to players who pull or slice the ball. The player's hips are now almost parallel to the target line, and his weight is primarily over the right foot.

After the downswing, Nick Faldo has moved his arms down while rotating his hips.

In this phase, a top golfer flexes his wrists towards the back of the hand (dorsal flexion) because this is the only way to form a small enough angle between the lower left arm and the back of the hand (for example, Ben Hogan). However, the handicap golfer should not waste any time at this point. Once you have started the downswing, as suggested, what follows happens almost automatically.

THE SWING

The club is again parallel to the ground and to the target line, travelling on its original plane.

Phase 6

During this phase, the player rotates the lower part of his body farther than the upper, and his shoulders are now almost parallel to the target line.

The angle of the right elbow joint also changes, so that the distance between the hands and the right shoulder increases.

As in the position during the backswing, the club is now parallel to the target line and the ground. You can clearly see this detail when watching golfers who always hit straight balls. If the angle here is too steep or too flat, the club hits through the ball from outside-in or inside-out, respectively. The relationship between the shoulders and the club must be correct. If, for instance, the shoulders point to the left of the target, the club (in relation to the body) is too flat, even if the club is parallel to the ground and the target line.

The left wrist is now in a straight line with the lower left arm. The weight of the clubhead, which follows the movement of the hands, causes the left wrist to bend towards the palm of the hand (volar flexion) and the right wrist to go into dorsal flexion. The lower right arm (viewed from the side) points directly to the ball.

Phase 7

Next, the player flexes his wrists towards the side of the little finger (ulnar flexion) and rotates the lower arms counterclockwise (left: supination; right: pronation). The movements take place just prior to the moment of impact.

The hands are in front of the ball at the moment of impact. The left wrist is in line with the lower arm.

The shaft is back in its original plane; hips point 30 degrees left of target; shoulders point almost straight at target.

THE SWING

The "release" of the left hand: the wrist starts flexing (ulnar flexion), the lower arm rotates . . .

We don't consider the volar flexion of the left wrist to be part of the basic movements. Since, even at the moment of impact, the hands are still ahead of the clubhead, the left wrist already bends in volar flexion. We need these three movements (lower-arm rotation, ulnar flexion, and volar flexion of the left wrist) in order to correctly "release" the club.

The golfer can practise in half swings, stopping the forward movement of the club immediately after the moment of impact. This allows the player a chance to see if the shaft is pointing towards the target line and is in a straight line with the left arm. The shoulders (viewed from the side) point towards the target or slightly to the left of it.

. . . clockwise (supination), and the wrist bends towards the palm of the hand (volar flexion).

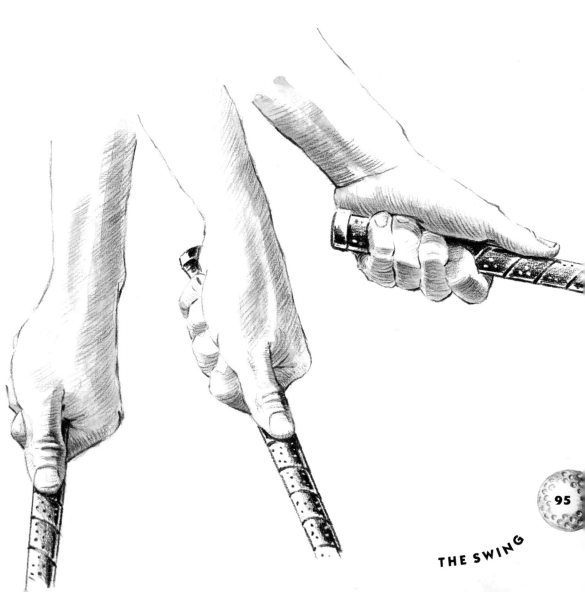

THE SWING

Moment of Impact

Looking at a player from the front, we can see a few differences between what happens at the moment of impact and in the address position.

The upper body tilts slightly to the right because the head is in the same position as it was in the address position, and the lower part of the body is comparatively farther to the right. This causes the left wrist to bend to the palm of the hand (volar flexion), allowing the player to swing the club down and through the ball. The club will lose some of its loft, which explains why some balls that start out low gain steadily in height during the flight, something that strong players do so well.

When compared to the address position, the player has rotated his hips to the left by approximately 30 degrees and moved them slightly in the direction of the target. The plane that it was in the address position. If an error should occur at this point, it is usually that the position of the handle is too high, causing the face of the club to point to the right, even if the leading edge is vertical to the target line. In this case, divots are almost always deeper on the outside than on the side closer to the golfer.

Usually, the reason for this mistake is that the plane of the shaft just prior to the moment of impact is too flat or that the club is swinging too steeply when it hits the ball. The latter forces the golfer to make himself taller, which places the end of the handle too high at the moment of impact as the golfer tries to prevent the clubhead from digging too deeply into the grass.

Free-wheeling

During the phase of the downswing in which the angle between the left arm and the club becomes larger (the release-point), the golfer should not try to increase the speed of the club by using additional force. This only slows the club down even more. The following might explain why this is so:

A biker wants to test the back wheel of his bike. He turns the bike upside down and cranks the pedals, making it turn at its maximum speed. He cannot increase the speed by turning the pedals even faster. In fact, any additional turning of the pedals only slows the wheel down. You can see an example of this free-wheeling principle by watching Ian Woosnam.

When learning the proper downswing, players have a hard time trying not to consciously guide certain movements, even after the release point. However, as soon as these movements become automatic, players should remember the principle of free-wheeling.

Scientific research has shown that the player must reduce the speed of the hands after the release point in order to maximize the speed of the clubhead. This contradicts the widely held notion that, during the downswing, players must steadily increase the force, from the beginning and up to the moment of impact, or, better yet, that the extra force needs to be used only during the second half of the swing.

How a Ball Becomes Airborne

In the course of my teaching, I am constantly reminded that very few golfers understand how a golf ball becomes airborne, so allow me to explain the principle involved.

The golfer must employ a special technique in order to get the ball into the air. He does not need to "spoon" the ball, which means that he does not need to be concerned if, at the moment of impact, the club is moving upwards and that his hands are behind the ball, trying to create an artificial plane. The reason for this is that golf clubs already have an angle of between 11 and 60 degrees.

When a player hits an iron correctly, the clubhead is already moving down, which makes a clean hit that much

When a player hits with an iron, the clubhead moves down through the ball, producing a divot to the left of the ball.

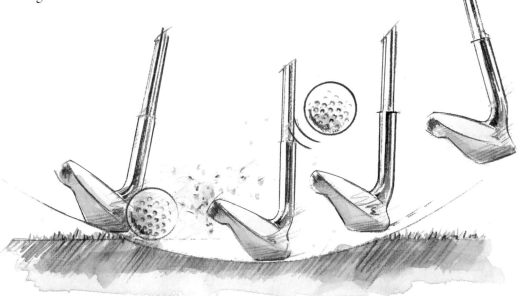

THE SWING

Bernhard Langer making an approach shot: in order to create as much backspin as possible, the club must swing down through the ball.

easier, particularly when the ball is in a difficult spot. A player does not need to move the clubhead under the ball, but rather from above, down and through the ball. Since many players are not clear about this process, they use incorrect spooning movements, particularly when hitting a high, short approach shot. Spooning the ball creates too much loft at the moment of impact (A-curve). The result is a weak hit that creates very little backspin.

This idea of "hitting down" holds true no matter which golf club the player uses, with two exceptions: when using a wood to tee off and when using a putter. A putter has almost no loft because a ball hit with a putter is not supposed to become airborne, and a slight upward movement when teeing off is possible because the ball is higher off the ground. Depending on the position of the ball, different downswings create different divots. The farther to the right the player places his ball and the shorter the club, the more pronounced the divots

you watch, pay attention to how a ball reacts after the club has hit a large divot: it falls immediately to the ground, and sometimes even rolls backwards. The vertical angle on impact is not the only factor. Equipment (club and ball), the speed of the clubhead, and a clean hit are also important. However, together with the loft of the club, the vertical angle con-

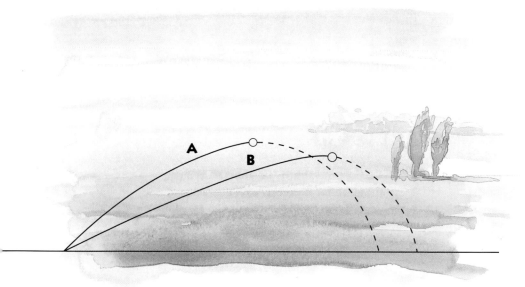

will be. With a long iron or wood, the club will only brush over the ground. Many people who watch golf competitions on TV wonder about the large divots that professional players produce.

But even if producing a large divot is not the ideal, it is still better than producing none at all. The next time

trols how quickly the ball will spin backwards. This backspin not only influences how quickly a ball comes to a stop after it hits the ground, it also makes the ball less sensitive to sidespins, as well as giving the ball a more stable flight and an optimal flight curve.

The steeper or flatter the angle with which the club hits the ball, the higher or lower the flight curve will be.

THE SWING

How does a player achieve a "downward" hit? The player has to bring the club to the ball correctly from the inside. If he hits the ball too far from the inside, the club is hardly able to hit through and down from above. A player uses a spooning movement, in which the clubhead approaches the ball from the outside, because he is instinctively trying to reduce the steep angle of the club at impact. Therefore, the player should keep his hands in front of the ball at the moment of impact. Also, it is important to remember that, in relation to the flexion of the wrists in the direction of the thumb, the follow-through is not a mirror image of the backswing. The right arm and the club (viewed from the front) are still in line long after the moment of impact. Only after the right arm is almost vertical to the ground does the player allow the club to move freely and the wrists to flex to the side of the thumb.

However, the player cannot hit down when his body weight is too far to the right at the moment of impact because this shifts the center of the swing to the right.

The Follow-Through

The follow-through is the phase that begins at the moment of impact and continues until the end of the swing. You might assume that the quality of this part of the swing is of little consequence since the ball is already on its way to the target. In reality, however, the follow-through has two important functions:
1. During this phase, the speed of the clubhead slows down enough to prevent any possibility of injury. In a properly executed, long follow-through, the head of the club will cover 270 degrees. The long braking phase resulting from it reduces the force and slows down the movement of the club.
2. The follow-through also influences the backswing. For instance, if a player stops his follow-through when the club reaches hip height, he not only increases the risk of injury but also starts to brake the forward movement of the clubhead prematurely, even before the moment of impact.

The follow-through is usually a good indicator of the quality of the movements that precede it. Look to the backswing, the posture, the stance, and even to the grip, if a player is not consistently successful in concluding his swing with a balanced end position. The first order of business should be to find the reason and correct the mistakes in those areas. With other problems taken care of, the follow-through usually improves all by itself.

A player should never attempt to steer the ball towards the target by influencing the movement of the club during or after the moment of impact. As we already discussed, this would contradict the principle of free-wheeling. It would slow down the club before the moment of impact, and it rarely produces the desired result.

I believe that the advice usually given to players, to swing the club in the direction of the target, is not very helpful because neither the clubhead nor the end of the handle is moving in the direction of the target during the backswing or the follow-through. This happens only during the fraction of a second at the moment of impact. Currently, many golf instructors try to correct as many mistakes as possible by changing the forward movements. In my opinion, they don't do enough work dealing with the causes. Of course, it is true that in that particular phase corrections are often easier to make and sometimes even bring the desired results; however, if the player does not correct the underlying mistakes (in the pre-shot routine or during a swing), he must constantly make changes throughout the forward movement. And then we could not possibly talk about an improvement of the swing, which really means simplifying it.

Phase 8

If the ball were not in the way, the moment when the club reaches its greatest speed would occur after the moment of impact. This happens when both arms are straight. The left arm and the club (viewed from the front) approximate a straight line. Only at this point does the angle between the left arm and the shaft dissolve (again, viewed from the front). The shaft (viewed from the side) is exactly in the original plane with the end of the handle pointing directly to the target line. As in Phase 1, the hands are inside (on the left side) of the clubhead. If the lower arms rotate too far counterclockwise, this won't be the case.

The club is still in its original plane. In relation to the curve of the swing, the clubface is closed.

*The left arm
and the club
shaft form
one straight
line. The
left wrist
and the lower
arm also form
one line.*

Until a few years ago, a great many players on the tour were moving to the ball from the extreme inside. Although this should have caused the ball to start out to the right, a very strong lower-arm rotation in the impact phase (strong draw) prevented it from doing so. However, few players use this technique today because the results are very unreliable.

As has already been mentioned, when released correctly, the hands are to the inside of the clubhead. The reason for this is not the extreme rotation of the shoulder or that the hands move too far to the left. This happens simply because the club is moving accurately on its plane. The left wrist and lower left arm are still in a straight line (viewed from the front). The wrists completely release to the side of the little fingers. The latter should not change during the next phase because it would make lower-arm rotation, which is independent of the body's movement, more difficult.

THE SWING

Phase 9

The club is again parallel to its original plane (below left).

In this phase, the end of the handle is closer to the ground than the clubhead. Once again, the shaft is parallel to the original plane of the club. The head of the club (viewed

ing slightly to the right of the goal, and the right arm is parallel to the ground.

Now the left elbow flexes, corresponding to the movement during the backswing. While in the latter case the

During the follow-through, the head of the club swings in an extremely wide arc (right).

from the front) travels a far greater distance than was the case during the backswing, because the wrists (in the corresponding position during the backswing) flex earlier.

The rotation has reached the point where the upper body is again in line with the lower body. The belt buckle and the chest bone are point-

left arm remains straight and the right elbow flexes, here the reverse occurs. The body now rotates completely around its left axis, and all of the player's weight shifts to the outside of the left foot. In Phase 9, the head has already turned so that the ball is directly in the player's line of vision. Trying to fix the eyes as long as possible on the spot where the ball has been isn't helpful. A golfer can't swing the club freely and far enough during the follow-through if he keeps looking down. And besides, bending the head down too long may cause back problems. A player doesn't have to be afraid that he will top the ball if he takes his eyes off it. To this day, I have never seen a golfer who has actually experienced this. In tennis, no one would think of looking at where the ball *was* after he hit the shot.

Even if your head has turned after you hit the ball, your body (viewed from the side) is still bending forward to the same degree. Therefore, at this point, your head has not moved up. In order to relieve some of the tension in your back, your upper body slowly begins to straighten up in the course of the swing.

Phase 10

During the last part of the swing, the player simply lets the speed of the club slow down naturally. The body rotates far enough so that the belt buckle points slightly to

the left of the target, and the right shoulder is closer to the target than the left. The upper part of the body is almost totally straight now. The player is standing completely upright (viewed from the front).

In the past, many golfers bent their upper bodies too far back, creating a reverse C.

The club is on a lower plane than before because the upper body has straightened up slightly.

105

To the untrained eye, this might look very athletic, but this happens because, at the moment of impact, the club is not moving down far enough and the player hollows his back, a very bad posture.

The upper body is perfectly vertical over the left leg.

Today, however, we often see players exaggerating the opposite way, bending their upper bodies too far forward. This means that the arms and the club have to try to catch up with the upper body, which has already moved ahead during the downswing. The result is usually a slice.

The right arm (viewed from the side) is parallel to the plane of the club, and the hands are to the left of the head. Because the upper body has straightened up slightly, the club is not parallel but slightly lower than its original plane.

The right wrist is now almost straight, and the left wrist has assumed dorsal flexion. This is the exact opposite of the position at the highest point in the backswing, where the right wrist had assumed dorsal flexion and the left wrists were almost straight. The wrists have turned completely towards the side of the thumbs. The right foot touches the ground only at the tip. The only contact that the left foot has with the ground is the heel and the outside of the shoe. The knees are close together.

In order to guarantee a fluid swing, a golfer should pay close attention to a correct, well-balanced end position. If, for instance, the player always falls back on his right foot at the end of the swing, he can be sure that his movement was wrong during the downswing and sometimes even earlier than that.

Learning the Swing

During discussions about the golf swing, we hear that the golfer should never think about or pay attention to technical details; rather, he should rely solely on how it feels. This might be good advice for children, who learn primarily through imitation, and for professional players, who already have a good command of the proper techniques. The average golfer, however, can't profit much from such advice. This makes as much sense as telling a beginning high jumper how to hold the pole and then telling him to just concentrate on getting over the bar. Even if it doesn't appear so at first sight, golf is a difficult sport. To be successful, the golfer has to carry out every movement correctly, just as the high jumper does.

However, the positions discussed in this book are only guidelines. You need not follow them absolutely and to the letter. But remember that the golf club and the golf ball only follow the law of mechanics. Disregarding this fact will have consequences on your game.

Many players never learn how to swing a golf club correctly because they get discouraged when a hit turns out poorly right after they have made corrections. They believe the corrections they made were wrong. But players are totally wrong when they think that every good hit is the result of a good swing, and every poor hit is the result of a bad one. Sometimes, two mistakes cancel each other out, and sometimes the original swing was correct and a previous compensation wasn't necessary.

Therefore, players should put less emphasis on hitting the ball well and pay more attention to executing the swing correctly.

The Principle of Exaggeration

When I am teaching, I frequently encounter the following phenomenon: After watching a video tape of his swing, a student has identified his problems and is perfectly ready to eliminate the causes. After only a few attempts, he is sure that he is in command of a swing that is completely new. He is very surprised when I tell him that the new swing is not any different from the old one.

To illustrate that you can't always trust your own feelings, here is an example that might be helpful: Imagine that you have been outside

THE SWING

for some time and that the temperature is 15° F (−10° C). After a while, you go into a building in which the temperature is 70° F (21° C). You will feel that it is very warm

The Swing

....

▶ The four basic movements of the backswing include: rotating the body, flexing the wrists, rotating the lower arms, and moving the arms away from the body. On the other hand, during the downswing, there are only two: moving the arms away from the body and rotating the body to the left (moving the hips to the side and the arms down).
▶ The club should be on or parallel to its original plane throughout the swing.
▶ The upper body rotates around the spine when (in the address position) bending forward.
▶ Except when you are teeing off, the club moves down and through the ball.

....

in the building. Now let's imagine that you have spent several days in the desert, where the temperature was 105° F (41° C). Go inside the same building where the temperature is 70° F (21° C), and that same 70° F (21° C) will feel awfully cold. This is an example of how we can't always trust our perceptions since our prior experiences always influence them.

The same holds true in golf. If your swings were very low, a normal swing will seem very extreme. Most players are not aware of this phenomenon, and so their corrections are too small. I often tell my students, "Make a correction in such a way that you feel as if you are really exaggerating the new move!" After several practice swings that the students think are absolutely and totally exaggerated, I show them a video. Usually they acknowledge that their perception misled them again and that the new swings were just about neutral. I can't state this idea of exaggeration often enough. Do not believe that you are an exception. Don't trust your feelings. As soon as you understand this and put it into practice, nothing will stand in the way of changing your swing successfully.

The Swing—In Short

Once you have mastered the prerequisites for the swing (grip, posture, stance, and pre-shot routine) and are able to use them consistently, don't lose sight of the overall objective by getting hung up on small details. When you carry out your movements according to the following basic principles, good hits will become the rule rather than the exception.

Backswing

At the start of the swing, move the club and the arms to the right. This will ensure that you will swing properly to the inside and up.

Since the upper body is rotating around a fixed axis (the spine) and against the hips, the shoulders rotate on a plane that is not as steep as that of the arms (parallel to the original plane of the remains parallel to the left lower arm, except during the moment of impact.

Make sure that you correctly carry out the movements that you are conscious of: pre-shot routine and backswing. The underlying, subconscious reactions make sure that the main part of the swing—the moment when the club actually hits the ball—will also be correct.

club). When the grip is correct, the weight of the clubhead tends to make the upward movement sluggish, causing the wrists to flex.

During all four basic movements, the club travels on the same plane it started out on, and it is parallel to the target line when it is parallel to the ground. The clubface always

Downswing

Ideally, the downswing is a matter of reflex because this movement is too fast to be consciously controlled. During the downswing, it makes sense to coordinate the "downswing" of the arms with the "moving-out-of-the-way" of the hips. Balls that start out to the left and then

veer off to the right do so because (assuming neutral preparations and backswing
movements) the upper body
rotates too fast. Balls that
start out to the right and then
veer off to the left do so because both the hands and the
arms were too fast.

One final note: In order for
your hits to be consistent and
successful, you should not
deviate too far from the basic
principles discussed in this
book, although there is always room for individual
characteristics and style.

THE SWING

APPENDICES

An effective and well-designed program to warm up is the best way to prepare your body and mind for the pressures of golf.

Warm-Ups

A sensible and useful program for warming up is as important for the golfer as it is for the athlete in any other sport. Unfortunately, the player who prepares himself before a game or a practice round is an exception.

A sprinter would not dream of parking his car, putting on his spikes, and immediately going to the starting blocks to run a 100-meter race. In golf, however, this seems to be the norm.

Most players reach for the 7 iron or for a wood, immediately trying to hit balls as far as possible. The few players who do some stretching be-

Exercise 1:
Turn your head alternately from left to right (do not rotate). Do not support this movement with your hands. This would put too much stress on your spine.

Exercise 2:
Alternately tilt your head from left to right. Each time, pull the opposite arm down without changing the position of your body.

fore they start swinging the club do it wrong. Traditionally, the movements they perform are not healthy for their backs, such as rotating the hips and bending down while swinging a golf club several times. Often these "preparations" include combinations of stretching and bouncing which overstretch tendons and ligaments. Proper warm-up prevents injuries (strains, muscle tears, spinal problems, etc.), increases the mobility of the joints, and improves overall body coordination. It also serves as a mental warm-up, helping the player to prepare mentally for

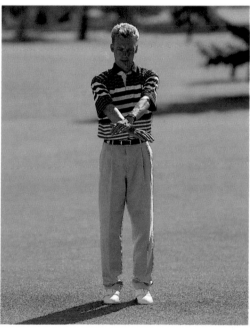

Exercise 3:
Move your shoulders forward and back. Alternately, keep your back straight and do not use a swinging motion.

Exercise 4:
Swing your arm to the sides and back. Start out slowly and do not use too much swinging motion.

the game and to increase training effectiveness.

Proper warm-up consists of four phases:

▶ The first is the *mobility* phase. This phase improves the cardiovascular system, increases blood circulation to the muscles, and warms up the joints, resulting in fluid motions. Carry out these movements slowly and smoothly. Perform each movement twice.

▶ The next step is *stretching*. Stretching is not a synonym

Exercise 5:
Place your right hand above your left elbow and begin to pull your body to the right. Do the same with your left hand and right arm, pulling your body to the left.

Exercise 6:
Stretch both arms in front of you. Push one hand down (with the palm pointing up) with the opposite hand. Repeat with the other hand.

for static muscle stretching. These movements prepare the musculature for the work that lies ahead. Proceed as follows:

First, slowly stretch the muscles until you can feel the pull. Hold this position 10 seconds. Release the tension for 5 seconds and stretch a bit farther until you can feel tension. Repeat this whole procedure twice.

▶ Next come *dynamic coordination exercises*. After the stretching exercises, the body needs to be prepared for the pres-

Exercise 7:
Turn your upper body from left to right, keeping your back straight and not moving your hips. Do this exercise slowly and without much momentum.

Exercise 8:
Grab your hand and stretch your arms straight overhead. Pull your body to the left and the right, always keeping your back straight.

sure that is to come. Coordination exercises start out slowly, increasing as they progress. Repeat these about 5 times.

► Conclude your warm-up program with *golf-specific exercises* (test swings). These include swinging the club with both feet next to each other, swinging the club like a baseball bat with the club in the address position about hip high, and reversing the normal swing, so that a right-hander swings like a left-hander and vice versa.

Exercise 9:
Place your feet next to each other and make three-quarter swings without losing your balance.

Exercise 10:
Hold the club the wrong way, so that a right-hander holds the club like a left-hander and vice versa, and take a few test swings.

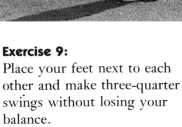

You will notice that your first hits are much more effective and successful when you have prepared yourself properly. When you start, you should begin with a wedge. Use half swings and do not look for longer hits until after you have completed at least 20 short hits. You should plan on at least 10 minutes of proper preparation. After you have finished, make sure to take time for some back exercises.

Exercise 11:
Hold the golf club out straight, parallel to the ground, and take a few baseball swings.

Exercise 12:
Bend one leg by moving your body forward. Rest your hands on the knee and stretch the other leg. Push the bent knee farther forward, but only far enough so that the foot of the stretched leg remains flat on the ground.

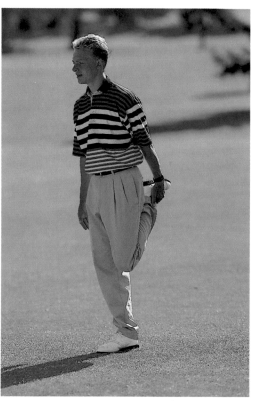

Make sure that your back is straight.

Exercise 13:
Reach behind you for your foot and pull it towards your body. Keep your pelvis upright and your thighs parallel to each other.

Glossary

Address position: The position of the golfer after having assumed his stance and positioned his club on the ground.

Angle at impact: The angle of the clubhead between the intended line to the target and the horizontal component of the path of the club just prior to impact. You can only observe this from the side. Ideally, the club hits through the ball inside-to-in. The force depends on the club: long club, more power; short club, less power. Possible deviations include:
1. The path of the curve moves outside-to-in.
2. The path of the curve moves inside-to-out (the horizontal angle at impact).

You can only view the angle between the ground and the vertical component of the path of the club immediately before impact from the front. Ideally, when using an iron, the club swings through the ball from above and down. When using a wood that is parallel to the ground and when teeing off with a wood, the club swings from below and up. This is the vertical angle at impact.

Angle of incidence: Overall term for the horizontal and vertical angle of impact.

Backspin: The rotation of the ball around its own axis against the direction of the flight. (Every ball in the air has a backspin, otherwise it would fall back to the ground immediately.) If the ball rolls back after it hits the ground, it has a particularly strong backspin. The loft of the club creates backspin.

Bulge: The horizontal plane on the clubhead that hits the ball.

Centrifugal force: The force that tends to push the ball away from the center of rotation.

Closed club: A clubface turned counterclockwise (viewed from the end of the handle). The terms "flat" and "steep" refer to the position of the shaft during the swing. The terms "open" and "closed" refer to the position of the clubface. The latter two terms are somewhat confusing, since "open stance" refers to the direction to the target, while "open clubface" refers to a club rotated to the right.

Dipping: A rotation of the shoulders towards a steep

121

plane. (The left shoulder is too low; the right shoulder is too high.)

Divot: A piece of grass cut out with a club.

Dorsal flexion: Bending the wrist in the direction of the back of the hand.

Downswing: The part of the swing starting at the end of the backswing to the moment of impact.

Fat hits: A shot in which the clubhead hits the ground in front of the ball. This shortens the length of the flight considerably.

Feedback: Without feedback (from video tape, computer analysis of the moment of im-pact, flight pattern of the ball, divot, feeling at the moment of impact, etc.) a player cannot accomplish any improvements.

Flat club: The club shaft (viewed from the side) oriented more horizontally than the lie would suggest.

Follow-through: The part of the swing from the moment of impact to the forward end position.

Forward movement: The part of the swing from the end of the backswing all the way to the follow-through.

Highest point of the swing: The highest point of the backswing, the point where the downswing begins.

Hook: A shot that starts out in the direction of the target and then veers to the left.

Iron Byron: A robot that simulates a golf swing, named after Byron Nelson, the golf pro. Almost all manufacturers of golf clubs and balls have such a robot.

Late hit: Occurs during the downswing when the angle between the lower left arm and the club shaft is late in dissolving.

Leading edge: The lower front edge of the clubhead.

Lie of the club: The angle between the shaft of the club and the sole of the club.

Loft: The angle of the club-face and the vertical line to the ground as the ball is lifted into the air.

Open club: The clubface turns clockwise (viewed from the end of the handle).

Plane: A golf swing has numerous planes, including the following:
1. The lie of the club defines the club plane.
2. The arm plane is the angle of the left arm (viewed from the side).
3. The shoulder plane is the angle created by the upper left and right sides of the shoulder during a swing (viewed from the side).
   In golf, a plane is flat when oriented horizontally and steep when oriented vertically.

Point of Release: The moment during the downswing when the angle between the left lower arm and the club begins to increase.

Pre-shot routine: A routine the player uses before starting the swing (grip, aim, trigger, waggle, etc.). Ideally, the player always follows the same sequence.

Pronation: The rotation of the lower arm in the direction of the side of the thumb.

Pull: A ball that starts out to the left and then flies straight.

Push: A ball that starts out to the right and then flies straight.

Radial flexion: Flexing the wrists in the direction of the thumb.

Release: Freeing the club (ulnar flexion, supination, and volar flexion to the left and pronation and dorsal flexion to the right) at the moment of impact.

Reverse C: The wrong end position of the swing in which the player's spine is bending into a reversed C (similar to creating a hollow back).

Slice: A ball that starts out in the direction of the target and then veers off to the right.

Steep club: A club shaft (viewed from the side) oriented more vertically than the lie would suggest. If the shaft were parallel to the ground, the end of the handle would be pointing to the left and the tip of the head to the right of the goal.

Supination: The rotation of

the lower arm towards the little finger.

Target line: The line between the ball and the target.

Thin hit: A shot in which the club hits the ball too high but still below the "equator." Such a hit has a flatter flight curve than a well-hit ball and usually has little backspin.

Trailing edge: The lower back edge of the clubhead.

Ulnar flexion: The rotation of the wrists in the direction of the palms.

Index

APPENDICES

Acknowledgments

Photographic use of equipment:
Mizuno (Germany) GmbH, Munich
Pro Shop of Oschberghof Golf Course and Club,
   Donaueschingen
Rolco Sport Products BV, Tilburg, The Netherlands
Bridgestone Sports Europe GmbH, Schwaben Market
Photo shoot locations:
Oschberghof Golf Course and Club, Donaueschingen
Stuttgart-Neckartal Golf Club

Credits

Photos: HARDT Sportphoto Int., Hamburg, pp. 9, 19,
   53, 62/63, 67, 91, 99, 113;
William Diesbrook, Neustadt: p. 3;
Atelier G&N Kohler, Leonberg, all others.
Artwork: CV&L, Kurt Dittrich, Miharbeit A.
   Schickert, Wiesbaden.

127